WELSH FOLLIES

SECRETS, STORIES AND SCANDALS

By the same author:

Walking with Welsh Legends:
   South-western Wales
   Northern Wales
   Central Wales
   South-eastern Wales
   North-eastern Wales

First published in 2015

© Text: Graham Watkins

ISBN: 978–1-84524-215-2

Cover design: Eleri Owen

Published by Gwasg Carreg Gwalch,
12 Iard yr Orsaf, Llanrwst, Conwy Wales LL26 0EH
Tel: 01492 642031   Fax: 01492 641502
email: books@carreg-gwalch.com
Website: www.carreg-gwalch.com

Welsh Follies

Secrets, Stories and Scandals

Graham Watkins

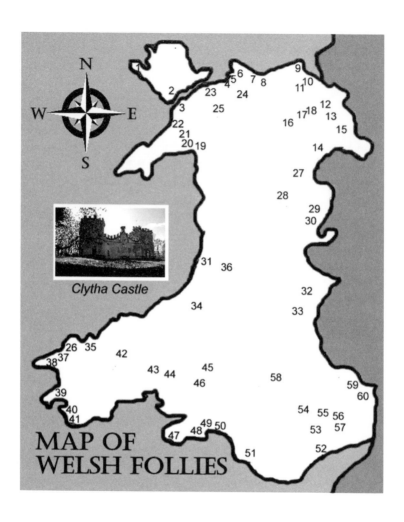

**MAP OF
WELSH FOLLIES**

N
W E
S

1
2
23
4 5 6 7 8
24
3
25
22
21
20 19

9
11 10
16 17 18 12
13
15
14
27
28
29
30

Clytha Castle

31
36
34
32
33

26 35
38 37
42
43 44
45
46
58
59
60
39
54 55 56
53 57
40
41
49 50
48
47
51
52

Contents

Introduction

*'Folly' n. a want of sense; weakness of mind;
irrationality; a foolish action; a useless and
needlessly extravagant structure.*

Welsh follies come in all shapes and sizes, from the
'Smallest House in Britain' on the quay at Conwy, once
the home of 6' 3" fisherman, Robert Jones, to Portmeirion
where, between 1925 and 1975, Sir Clough Williams-
Ellis constructed follies on an epic – almost industrial –
scale. In building Portmeirion, Williams-Ellis produced
one of the most extravagant and beautiful follies in the
world. In the 1960s his Italianate creation was used as
the location for the cult television programme *The
Prisoner*. Today, Portmeirion is a popular tourist
attraction visited by thousands of people every year. But
it is a folly with a vision. Clough Williams-Ellis created
Portmeirion in order to show how even an area of great
natural beauty might be developed without spoiling it.
He believed that architecture should enhance the
landscape and hoped that at Portmeirion this could be
demonstrated in practice. With luck perhaps this
experiment might also inspire others to take an interest
in the environment and even motivate them to share his
lifelong struggle for the preservation of the countryside
against the excesses of uncontrolled development.
  Like the Irish famine follies of the 1840s, some Welsh
follies were built to provide a means of sustenance for
hungry men. *Tŵr y Deri* (Derry Ormond Tower), built

7

near Lampeter (*Llanbedr Pont Steffan*) in 1837 on the orders of a local squire, is one example. The squire wanted to provide employment for the men of Betws Bledrws. Other follies were built as ornaments by wealthy landowners, monuments to their vanity, or as exclamation marks placed on the land to record often forgotten historical events. Some Welsh follies are eccentric, many are curious, pretending to be something that they aren't, while others have a more serious purpose, but all have a story to tell.

This book explores the stories behind sixty curious and often apparently pointless buildings in Wales. We might call them 'follies', but here you can discover who built them, why they were built and what the people involved in creating these architectural oddities were trying to achieve. Learn why Morgan Jones built an elaborate house of shells in Pembrokeshire, and what William Paxton was trying to prove when he built a strange Gothic tower in Carmarthenshire.

'By God, Sir, I've lost my leg!' cried Henry Paget, when his leg was shot away at the Battle of Waterloo. His heroism and capacity for fun, despite being an invalid after the war, made him famous while his severed leg became a tourist attraction visited by royalty. Paget's exploits are commemorated on Anglesey by one of the tallest follies in Wales.

Further south, in Roath Park, Cardiff (*Caerdydd*), there is a peculiar clock tower, surrounded by a boating lake, with a strange connection with the South Pole.

Some apparently pointless follies are significant monuments. One of these is the Hallelujah Obelisk, built in a remote field by a local farmer to commemorate a battle which few have heard about, even though it changed the course of Welsh history. Others are less important. John Renie, a painter and decorator, carved his own gravestone, intending to trick the devil and save his soul. Renie died in 1832. Whether his plan worked is not known, but the headstone, which still stands in St Mary's Churchyard, Monmouth, is an impressive puzzle.

A more imposing folly is the Pin Mill at Bodnant, a building that few people know has been recycled three times and was once a store containing animal hides.

When Winifred Bamford-Hesketh discovered her husband was a philanderer, she changed her will and left Castell Gwrych, an enormous folly built by her grandfather, to the Prince of Wales. After she died, her angry husband took his revenge with a calculated act of vandalism.

Less damaging was the game that Major Walter Wingfield invented at Nantclwyd Hall, Ruthin (*Rhuthun*). Today we know it as lawn tennis.

Why did Rocky Marciano, an American who became heavyweight boxing champion of the world, live in Jersey Marine Tower, a Welsh folly in Swansea (*Abertawe*)?

These are just a few examples of the stories revealing, as they do, the history of our bizarre buildings while bringing to life interesting characters and events from our past. While I cannot guarantee the certainty of every tale, many have become part of folklore and legend and I'm confident that all are based on real events.

Researching the history of Welsh follies has been

enjoyable and I owe particular thanks to my cousin Graham Watkins for his suggestions, and my wife Patricia, who took most of the photographs.

The passing of time has been unkind to a number of the follies. Prospect Tower, once a lovely Gothic building, is now surrounded by modern houses, its windows shuttered with ugly plywood boards and now the permanent home of a rare species of bat. The folly is a listed building but the bats have even more conservation rights. Others, like Gnoll Belvedere, are a ruin. More fortunate follies have fared better. The Pin Mill at Bodnant has been rescued and lovingly rebuilt. Bryncir Tower is now a stunning high-rise holiday cottage, while Jersey Marine Tower has been restored to become a luxury bridal suite, the centrepiece of the Towers Hotel.

A few of the architects who built our follies might be thought of as being weak of mind or irrational, and some of the follies can be described as useless or needlessly extravagant. Despite being odd – and some follies certainly are – they all add to our rich culture and the history that is part of Welsh heritage. Best of all, discovering Welsh follies is great fun.

Graham Watkins
2015

Ellin's Tower
Anglesey

In 1553, during the reign of Edward VII, John ap Owen was granted land at Penrhos, Holy Island (*Ynys Gybi*), off the north-western corner of Anglesey (*Ynys Môn*). He went on to create a dynasty that would become the most powerful family on the Island for the next 400 years. Being politically active and willing to marry into money strengthened the family's financial position. While the male side of the Owen family sometimes lacked drive and strength of character, a succession of powerful women compensated for the weakness. Margaret Owen, born in 1742, was said to be a particularly masterful character. She married Sir John Thomas Stanley, who was descended from a prominent Derby family, whereupon the estate passed to the Stanley line.

The Stanleys of Derby were an interesting bunch. One became a Muslim and built a mosque at Talyboilon, while another became the Dean of Westminster Cathedral. Different branches of the family became the Barons of Alderley and the Earls of Sheffield; others became politicians.

William Owen Stanley, born in 1802, served as a captain in the Grenadier Guards before becoming the Member of Parliament for Anglesey. He was also a keen antiquarian, recognised as an authority on Celtic

Ellin's tower viewed from the south with South Stack lighthouse beyond. Ellin's Tower is now used by the RSPB and is open to the public

artefacts and a contributor to archaeological magazines. William married Ellin Williams and the family continued to live at Penrhos.

The crenellated clifftop folly, at South Stack, was built for Ellin in 1868 as a summerhouse where the family could enjoy the sea air and spectacular views. William Owen Stanley went on to serve as Lord Lieutenant of Anglesey and lived at Penrhos until he died in 1884.

During the Second World War, the estate was commandeered by the authorities and the house occupied by the military. When peace broke out, the house, which had been badly neglected by the army, was sold off, together with the estates farmland covering several thousand acres. Attempts were made to restore the house but it was eventually demolished. In 1969, 500 acres of farmland, once part of the estate, was sold for the development of Anglesey Aluminium's smelting plant and in 1972 the company granted the public access to the land. Since then it has been used as a country park and administered by Kehoe Countryside Limited for the enjoyment of the general public and the benefit of wildlife.

Ellin's tower was refurbished and opened in 1982 as an RSPB seabird centre. Since then, it attracts thousands of visitors every year. It is said that on a clear day it is possible to see the Irish Mountains of Mourne and the Isle of Man from the tower's observation room. South Stack is a stunning location and the white tower that balances precariously on the cliff edge is perfect for bird-watchers. According to the RSPB website more than 4,000 birds visit the area each year, while seals and dolphins are regularly seen in the waters below the tower. As well as being able to watch the seabirds through high-powered binoculars provided by the RSPB, there are webcam links to nests containing chicks, and interactive displays to inform those who want to learn more about the wildlife inhabiting the rocky coastline.

The Royal Commission of Ancient and Historical Monuments of Wales have described Ellin's Tower as 'A post-medieval, dour, castellated clifftop folly, built in the form of a toy castle, commanding spectacular views to seaward'. The description is honest, but a little unfair to a lovely folly which today serves a very practical purpose and gives pleasure to thousands of visitors.

2

The Marquess of Anglesey's Column
Anglesey

Take the Britannia Bridge across the Menai Strait to the Island of Anglesey (*Ynys Môn*) at the northernmost part of Wales and you cannot help notice the magnificent column ahead of you. The 27-metre-tall column thrusts itself skyward near the village of Llanfair Pwllgwyngyll. A Victorian resident, however, attempting to lure tourists to the area in the 1860s, created a rather longer name, which, containing fifty-eight letters, is the longest place name in Britain. 'Llanfairpwllgwyngyllgogerychwyrndrobwllllantysiliogogogoch translates as 'St. Mary's Church in a hollow of white hazel near the swirling whirlpool of the church of St. Tysilio with a red cave.' The locals normally shorten the name to Llanfair Pwllgwyngyll (or Llanfair P.G.).

On Sunday 18 June 1815, an army commanded by the Duke of Wellington defeated Napoleon Bonaparte's French army and ended his rule as Emperor of France. The column at Llanfair P.G. commemorates the battle, and the bronze statue standing on the top represents Henry Paget, 2nd Earl of Uxbridge, an heroic soldier who made his name as one of Wellington's officers. The battle lasted most of the day and Paget was in the thick of the action. Early in the day he led a charge of heavy cavalry that severely weakened the French centre. Later Paget was mounted on his horse near Wellington when part of his leg was shot away by cannon fire and he is reputed to have exclaimed 'By God, sir! I have lost my leg.'

To which the Duke is said to have replied, 'By God, sir! So you have.'

The Earl was carried to a house in the village of Waterloo where the rest of the leg was amputated. During the operation, which was carried out without any aesthetic,

The Marquis of Anglesey's tower with fine views from the top

Paget apparently commented, 'The knives seem somewhat blunt'. According to an account written by Henry Curling, just after the surgeon had taken off the leg, Sir Hussey Vivian came into the cottage where the operation was performed.

'Ah, Vivian!' said the wounded noble, 'I want you to do me a favour. Some of my friends here seem to think I might have kept that leg on. Just go and cast your eye upon it, and tell me what you think.'

'I went, accordingly,' said Sir Hussey, 'and, taking up the lacerated limb, carefully examined it and, so far as I could tell, it was completely spoiled for work.

A rusty grape-shot had gone through and shattered the bones all to pieces. I therefore returned to the Marquis and told him he could set his mind quite at rest as his leg, in my opinion, was better off than on.'

Five days after the battle Henry Paget was created Marquess of Anglesey and offered a pension of £1,200 a year. He accepted the elevation to Marquess but refused the pension. Recognising a business opportunity, the owner of the house where the leg had been amputated, a Monsieur Paris, retained the leg and buried it in his back garden, where he built a tomb for the limb, which he charged visitors to view. The leg became a profitable business for the Paris family, with curious tourists from across Europe calling to see the shrine of the now famous leg. Visitors included the King of Prussia and the Prince of Orange.

Asked, after the amputation, how he felt, the Earl would reply, 'I feel like I have one foot in the grave'. Losing his leg did not slow the Marquess down. He had an artificial leg made which hinged at the knee. He was known to enjoy dancing, went on to reach the rank of Field Marshal, and lived until he was eighty-five, passing away in 1854.

In 1878 the Marquess' son visited M. Paris' house and was horrified to discover the leg bones had been dug up and were now on open display. He demanded the return of his father's leg but refused to pay the extortionate price claimed by the Paris family. A diplomatic row was averted when the Belgian authorities instructed that the leg be reburied. In 1934, when the last Monsieur Paris died, his widow discovered that the bones had not been reburied, as ordered, but instead were hidden in her house. To avoid any further fuss she incinerated the remains in her central heating boiler.

If you are feeling energetic you can visit the tower, pay a small entrance fee, and climb the 115 narrow steps that take you up the inside of the column to a viewing platform near the top where there are stunning views of the Menai Strait. The Marquess' country seat, Plas Newydd, now a National Trust property, is nearby. His artificial leg is on display, and there is also more information about this extraordinary man's life.

3

Castell Bach
Caernarfon

The Thomas family of Coed Helen can be traced back to Sir William Thomas, Sheriff of Carmarthenshire, in the sixteenth century. His son Rice was appointed to survey Crown lands in north Wales, and moved north where he met and married Jane Puleston, a widow from Caernarfon. His position enabled him to acquire two lucrative manors in 1553, which became the start of a family fortune. Rice Thomas went on to become the Sheriff of both Anglesey and Caernarfonshire.

In 1601 Rice's son William borrowed money to purchase 'Koydalen', an estate to the west of Caernarfon. During the next 300 years the family went through financial ups and downs but managed to retain Koydalen. By the nineteenth century another Rice Thomas was the master and the estate's name had changed to Coed Helen. Rice served as Sheriff of Caernarfonshire from 1831 to 1832 and was described as a quiet country gentleman. Not much more can be said about him except that he built Castell Bach (*castell*: castle; *bach*: small) on the hill overlooking Caernarfon, possibly as a summer house where he could enjoy the splendid views across the Menai Strait.

Rice Thomas died in 1859, without producing an

heir. His sister Elizabeth inherited the estate. She married Sir William Bulkeley Hughes from Angelesey and produced a son, Rice Robert Hughes, who became a clergyman. He died in 1850 and his son, another Rice, inherited Coed Helen when he was just nine years old. The boy changed his name to Rice Williams Thomas, grew up, married and moved away. After his departure, little is known about who occupied Coed Helen.

Castell Bach – today, it's a mobile phone tower

Today, Coed Helen has been rebranded as 'White Tower' and is a large static caravan park. Castell Bach stands alone and dejected on a hill. Despite the apparent neglect and grafitti, Castell Bach still serves a useful purpose. The crumbling masonry has been reinforced with a steel frame and the tower has been crowned with unsightly communications antenna.

4

Crow's Nest Farm
Conwy

In 1760, the Prime Minister, William Pitt, stated:

> The poorest man may in his cottage bid defiance to all the force of the Crown. It may be frail, its roof may shake the wind may blow through it. The rain may enter. The storms may enter. But the king of England may not enter. All his forces dare not cross the threshold of the ruined tenement.

It wasn't a new idea. That a man's home was his castle had been enshrined in common law as far back as the thirteenth century. If Pitt had been looking for a good example of a defiant cottager, Crow's Nest Farm would have been the ideal residence.

The history of the tiny house near Conwy is unclear, but its construction is unusual. One half of the single-storey structure is covered by a sloping tiled roof, while the other supports a stubby castellated tower, ideal for pouring boiling oil on unwanted visitors.

A householder's right to refuse entry continued unchallenged until 2004 when a Labour government introduced legislation to allow forced entry to recover unpaid fines. In 2007, bailiffs were given the right to use physical force to pin down and restrain obstructing home owners. Today, towers and

Crow's Nest Farm, a modest but splendid building

battlements would not stop the legions of people with authority to enter without permission. These include policemen, firemen, the revenue, bailiffs, gas and electricity suppliers, an estimated 20,000 authorised council officials and planning inspectors checking for any unauthorised development. According to the Home Office, there are 1,043 different laws that allow inspectors to enter without permission. The Bees Act allows inspectors to search for foreign bees. Your home can be searched for illegal tattoo parlours, artificial human egg fertilisation laboratories or, strangely, offences related to stage hypnotism. According to Big Brother Watch, defenders of civil liberties, inspectors have even been authorised to enter homes to check the efficiency ratings of electrical appliances. Any attempt to remove a bailiff from a property is considered an assault and liable to prosecution. To add insult to injury, they have the power to charge the debtor a fee for each visit, and add another charge to cover the cost of removing any goods seized. Mindful of 'over-enthusiastic' bailiffs, the courts have set some limits on how bailiffs can operate, but more rights of entry will undoubtedly follow.

William Pitt's words are, sadly, no longer correct. Today, no man's home is his castle and the poor man in his cottage can no longer bid defiance to the forces of the Crown. Equally sadly, Crow's Nest Farm has been left to deteriorate and is in a very sorry state, but it's a fun building and whoever built it created a rather splendid little dwelling.

5

The Smallest House
Conwy

Queen Elizabeth I was on the throne when a rather unusual house was built in Conwy. To keep costs down, the builder wanted a site where three outside walls already existed, and found what he wanted on the quayside. Buildings had been erected along the medieval town walls, but there was a small gap left and it was here that the house was built. Using existing outside walls may have been economic, but since the gap the house was squeezed into was rather small the result was a very little house. The dwelling was so small that, following an advertising campaign by an enterprising local newspaperman, Robert Dawson, and extensive enquiries throughout the land, the house has been recognised by the Guinness Book of Records as the smallest house in Britain.

Quay House, as it is known, is 10 feet (3 metres) by 6 feet (1.8 metres), and despite having two storeys is just 10 feet 2 inches tall. The last occupant of the house was a local fisherman by the name of Robert Jones who, being 6 feet 3 inches (1.9 metres) tall, must have found the living conditions rather cramped. There was nowhere he could stand up in the house. It might have been for this reason that Mr Jones was said to have spent most of his time, when he wasn't at sea, in the local taverns. Locally, there is

The Smallest House, closed in February
but a popular tourist attraction
during the summer

a tradition that he slept with the bedroom window open – with his feet on the window sill! On 15 May 1900 Mr Jones was forced to move out when the local authority condemned the house as unfit for human habitation. There was nothing structurally wrong with the house but its lack of a toilet gave the authority an excuse to remove the fisherman. Without the intervention of the local paper, anxious to promote the town and recognising a good story, the smallest house in Britain would then have been demolished.

Because of the publicity the house received, visitors began to ask to have a look inside and were charged one old penny for the briefest of tours. To make more money Mr Jones had postcards produced of himself and his wife, in Welsh costume, standing outside the house. These he sold as souvenirs.

Today, the house, which is still owned by descendants of Mr Jones, is a popular tourist attraction, open to the public in the summer months. For a small fee, paid to a lady dressed in Welsh costume, visitors can peer inside, clamber up a ladder to look at the tiny bedroom, and read about the house in seventeen different languages.

The Smallest House,
closed in February
but a popular tourist
attraction during
the summer

6

The Bodysgallen Obelisk
Conwy

Bodysgallen Hall has a long and distinguished history. According to tradition, the site was the home of Cadwallon Lawhir (*llaw*: hand; *hir*: long), a ruler of north Wales during the fifth century. According to the medieval poet, Iolo Goch, 'Cadwallon's arms were so long he could reach a stone from the ground, to kill a raven, without bending his back because his arms were so long.' Cadwallon was murdered by his nephew, Maelgwn Gwynedd, who then claimed the throne for himself.

The *Records of Caernarvon* tell us that a watchtower existed at Bodysgallen in the thirteenth century, its purpose being to act as a lookout point for Conwy castle. During Elizabethan times, Bodysgallen belonged to Richard Mostyn, High Sheriff of Caernarfonshire and his family motto '*Auxilium Meum a Domino*' (the Lord is my help) is inscribed above the fireplace in the great hall.

By the seventeenth century, Bodysgallen had passed, when Margaret Mostyn married Hugh Wynn, to the Wynn family whose lineage stretches back to the House of Aberffraw and Rhodri the Great. Branches of the Wynn family owned much of north Wales. One possible relative, thought by Sir John Wynn, the first Baronet, to have been a family member born 'on the wrong side of the blankets', was the outlaw Twm Siôn Cati.

In 1620, Robert and Katherine Wynn extended the hall and had their initials carved on a date stone on the south-west gable end. They also added the walled gardens and a formal garden in the Dutch style, which was popular at the time. During the next 156 years the Wynn family expanded and improved Bodysgallen. A kitchen wing was built in 1730. The last of the male line, Dr Hugh Wynn, died in 1771, having added the north-east

Bodysgallen Obelisk, a huge modern folly that has upset the neighbours

wing to the house. It then passed to his daughter Margaret. In 1776 Margaret Wynn married Sir Roger Mostyn, 5th Baronet, returning Bodysgallen Hall back to the Mostyn family.

In 1832, one of the first water closets was installed at Bodysgallen, purchased from a Mr Williams of St Asaph. Towards the end of the nineteenth century, various extensions to the house had created a muddle of a building. Lady Augusta Mostyn took on the responsibility for restoring and simplifying the style of the hall. Her son Colonel Henry Mostyn raised the 17th Battalion of Royal Welch Fusiliers and paraded them at Bodysgallen Hall before they departed for the trenches of the First World War. The Royal Welch Fusiliers were involved in ferocious fighting at the Battle of the Somme and Mametz Wood, where they lost 4,000 men after officers ordered them to walk slowly uphill, straight into the line of fire.

An oak tree standing in the park commemorates the parade.

Henry Mostyn's eccentric son, Ieven, inherited Bodysgallen in 1949 but showed little interest in the Hall.

By 1969 Bodysgallen had deteriorated and was sold to be used as a guest house. During the 1980s, major restoration work was undertaken and Bodysgallen opened as an 'Historic House Hotel,' a brand owned and managed by the National Trust. Generally the restoration and improvements to Bodysgallen were well received, but on 30 August 1993 a disagreement was exposed when the *Independent* newspaper ran a story about the new hotel. Its owner, Richard Broyd, had submitted a series of planning applications to Aberconwy District Council, regarding the renovations, which they approved without noticing a rather significant proposal buried in the detail.

Residents of the village of Pydew were horrified when an enormous obelisk was erected on Ffrith Hill. Ffrith Obelisk Action Group was formed to have the blot on the landscape removed. A 700-word petition was produced. North Wales Wildlife Trust and Snowdonia National Park added their support to the campaign. The Countryside Council for Wales, who advised on the planning application, wrote to the action group saying, 'The location of the proposed obelisk . . . was not properly recognised by CCW, so there did not appear to be any significant implications for nature conservation interests.'

Bill Brice, chairman of the planning committee, admitted, 'The obelisk is too big and the site is too prominent. Recently we turned down a small extension to a house nearby because it would break the skyline. Yet this has been allowed and its sole purpose is to dominate the skyline. It should definitely never have been built.'

Because of the ineptitude of the planning authorities, a monstrous 64 foot (20 metre) obelisk had been built on a prominent hill and there was little that could be done about it. Mr Broyd was within his rights and would be entitled to compensation if forced to dismantle the folly. Mr Broyd refused to back down and threatened to fight in the courts, if need be. Twenty years later, the obelisk still stands, dominating the skyline to the east of Conwy; proof, if ever it was needed, of the inadequate nature of planning controls.

Tan y Coed
Colwyn Bay

Sir Charles Woodall, a shipping tycoon from Manchester, lived in Tan y Coed Hall, Colwyn Bay (*Bae Colwyn*) during the nineteenth century. He was a passionate pipe-smoker, a habit that his wife thoroughly disapproved of. When she banned him from smoking in the house, the magnate decided to build a sanctuary where he could escape from being nagged and puff away contentedly.

The unusually-shaped refuge was completed in 1894. Sir Charles' new smoking room was a three-sided folly castle complete with corbelled turrets and arrow slits, presumably to deter his wife should she try and visit.

After Sir Charles had departed, the folly was converted into a café and sweet shop. During the Second World War, Tan y Coed folly was occupied by the military and used to watch for enemy aircraft. No longer needed when the war ended, it was boarded up and forgotten.

Tan y Coed Hall was demolished in the 1970s and the surrounding land developed for housing. In 1991, a campaign was started to save the by then derelict mock castle. A year later, Clwyd Historic Buildings Preservation Trust purchased the folly for £1 and spent a further £65,000 restoring it, their plan being

Tan y Coed, a smoker's retreat built to escape a nagging wife

to sell it afterwards as a house.

Today, Tan y Coed folly castle stands in a small municipal garden, surrounded by modern houses. Viewed from the road, the medieval style folly is an attractive building and it is easy to imagine Sir Charles relaxing inside while enjoying his pipe.

Castell Gwrych
Abergele

In the nineteenth century, Gothic revival architecture was the height of fashion. The new Houses of Parliament were built in the Gothic style between 1836 and 1865. Anglican churches were decorated using Gothic designs, and wealthy Victorians wanted Gothic houses. Turrets, steeply-pitched roofs, pointed arches, gargoyles and stained glass windows were a must; the exuberant ostentation, intended to suggest a romantic past, came to be described as High Victorian Gothic.

When, in 1819, Lord Hesketh Bamford-Hesketh wanted a new country house near Abergele, it was natural that it would be built in the Gothic style. The old Elizabethan house he was replacing was soon demolished and work started on the new one. Leading architects were commissioned to oversee the project. No expense was to be spared; Lord Hesketh wanted to demonstrate his wealth. Gwrych estates included more than 6,000 acres, extended across northern Wales, Cheshire, Lancashire and Derbyshire. It took more than ten years to complete the house. By 1825, when Lord Hesketh married Lady Emily Ester Ann Lygon, the main house was complete.

Although Castell Gwrych was already a substantial property, building continued after the marriage.

Castell Gwrych, possibly the biggest folly in the world

During the 1840s a new wing containing bedrooms was built. New staircases and porches were added. The cabinet-maker George Bullock crafted bespoke furniture; Graces, interior furnishers to the nobility, provided the fittings.

When Lord Hesketh died in 1861, Castell Gwrych passed to his son, Robert Bamford-Hesketh. Robert, like his father, had the building bug, but the cost of building such an enormous house had consumed a lot of money. Nearly half the estate had been sold to fund construction. Only 3,400 acres remained. Fortunately for Robert, shafts sunk on the estate's land revealed rich seams of coal and a number of mines were soon producing good returns. Robert used the money to extend Castell Gwrych, including adding a private chapel. The residents of Abergele watched in wonder as castellated walls punctuated with turrets and towers spread across the side of the hill. Gwrych now resembled a vast, romantic, Camelot-style fairytale castle.

Robert's development of Gwrych ended with his death in 1894 when his daughter Winifred inherited the estate and castle. Winifred Bamford-Hesketh took up residence at Gwrych with her husband Douglas Hamilton Cochrane, 12th Earl of Dundonald. The new family soon made themselves at home, were quickly accepted as prominent members of the community and went on to have five children. The earl was a military man and spent time in South Africa during the Boer War where he commanded a mounted brigade which took part in the relief of Ladysmith. During the First World War, he was the Chairman of the Admiralty Committee on Smoke Screens.

Despite outward appearances, the union between Winifred and her husband was not always a happy one. Some accounts suggest the marriage had been arranged and that the earl had conducted a series of illicit liaisons with other women. Winifred thrust herself into Welsh affairs and was a founding member of the Church in Wales. When Winifred was herself implicated in a relationship with the Archbishop of Wales the marriage broke down.

In 1924, Winifred died and in doing so took her revenge on her estranged husband. She bequeathed Gwrych Castle to George, Prince of Wales, ostensibly to give the royal family a permanent residence in Wales. The prince, who would later become King George V, refused the legacy; possibly not wanting to get involved in a family dispute. Instead, ownership of the castle, and what was left of the estate, passed to The Venerable Order of St John. The order did not keep Gwrych for long. In 1928, the Earl of Dundonald repurchased the castle for £78,000 and then, in a vengeful act of vandalism, stripped its fittings and sold them to cover the cost.

Douglas Hamilton Cochrane, 12th Earl of Dundonald, died in 1935 and his son Thomas assumed the title 13th Earl of Dundonald. Gwrych, with its rambling mock castle walls and empty chambers, was no longer a family home and in 1946 Thomas sold the castle for £12,000. During World War II, the authorities requisitioned Gwrych and used it to shelter 200 Jewish refugees.

In 1948, businessman Leslie Salts bought the castle and opened it as a tourist attraction. He branded Gwrych as 'The Showplace of Wales' and was soon doing good business. Salts ran Gwrych for twenty years and is said to have received more than 10 million visitors. The Castle changed hands again in 1968 and the new owners continued to operate it as a tourist attraction. Medieval jousting matches were held. The library was converted into a bar and the dining room was used for mock banquets. Boxers including Randolph Turpin and Bruce Woodcock used Gwrych for their training camps, and motorcycle rallies were held in the grounds. Despite such events, the castle went into decline and, after changing hands a number of times, closed to the public in 1985.

Since then vandalism, weather and absentee owners have left Gwrych Castle a crumbling ruin.

Most of the internal floors and the roofs have rotted away and the once grand castle is at risk of becoming structurally unsound. Attempts have been made to save the Grade I listed building. American businessman Nick Travaglione paid £750,000 for the castle in 1989 and announced he was going to turn it into a five star hotel and opera house. His plans came to nothing and the castle continued to rot. In 2006 it was sold again to Clayton Hotels who had similar ideas.

The new owners then spent a further £500,000 cleaning up the castle before going into receivership.

In 2010, the administrators sold the castle to Edwards Property Management (UK) Ltd. of Colwyn Bay for £300,000. In the same year, the *Sun* newspaper carried a lead story about a photograph that had been taken at the castle. When the picture was developed the faint image of a woman peering out from the banqueting hall window was revealed but, with no floor inside the building to support someone, she could not have been there. 'Screamy Window' ran the headline and described Gwrych as the most haunted building in Britain. Other ghosts, odd occurrences and strange deaths have also been recorded at Gwrych. Was the apparition Winifred's ghost, wandering through the room of her now derelict castle?

Today, the plans to develop Gwrych as a leisure complex are still with the planning authorities and the castle may yet return to its former magnificence.

9

Talacre Lighthouse
Talacre

From early times the river Dee (*Dyfrdwy*) has been a major trade route. The Roman garrison at Chester was supplied by seagoing vessels. Ships carrying goods from Ireland, Spain and Germany used the Dee Estuary to shelter from unfavourable winds. During the Industrial Revolution traffic along the river increased dramatically. In 1737 a new channel was cut to improve navigation and in 1777 a lighthouse was built at the Point of Ayr to guide ships into the estuary. Situated on the most northerly point of the Welsh mainland, Point of Ayr was the earliest lighthouse to be built in Wales. Records show that Edward Price, the first lighthouse-keeper, was paid an annual salary of sixteen guineas for his duties.

The original lighthouse fell into the sea and was replaced in 1819 by the structure that stands, like a sentinel, on Talacre Beach today. The tower that rises out of the sand is 18 metres (58 feet) tall, and on a clear night the light could be seen from 19 miles away. Census records show that many of the keepers lived in the lighthouse with their wives and children. In 1841, the keeper, Samuel Brooks, his wife and three children lived there, together with keeper Richard Hughes. At the time of the next census in 1851, ten years later, both men were still stationed at the Point of Ayr lighthouse.

Talacre Lighthouse marooned, high and dry at low tide

Other lighthouse keepers at Talacre were single men and, for them, the life of a keeper could a lonely one. In 1844, while Samuel Brook was the keeper, a new, pile lighthouse was built offshore and the Talacre Beech lighthouse became redundant. Not long after it was closed, strange things began to happen. Visitors to the beach would report seeing a man dressed in a frock coat cleaning the lighthouse lantern. But, when the lighthouse was searched no one was there and the door leading to the tower was secured with stout chains and padlocks. There were more sightings of the ghostly lighthouse keeper. People who approached the lighthouse complained of feeling ill and uneasy as if an evil spirit was watching them. Whole families were struck down with sickness. Dogs walking with their owners ran away and cowered, refusing to approach the lighthouse.

As the paranormal reputation of Talacre lighthouse spread, ghost hunters arrived to search for phantom spirits. Some said the ghost of a long dead lighthouse keeper, unable to light the lamp to warn passing ships, kept a lonely vigil at the top of the tower. Others, more sceptical, scoffed at such nonsense and said the apparitions were a reflection through the lens and nothing more than a trick of the light.

During the Second World War, Talacre lighthouse was used as an observation post and reports of the ghostly keeper stopped. But, at the end of the war, with the lookout post no longer needed, the lighthouse was abandoned and sealed once more. Not long after, sightings began again of a strange man, dressed in old fashioned clothes, at the top of the lighthouse. A couple on holiday watched the man for some time. A family from Hereford started to take photographs by the lighthouse when then began to feel uneasy. Four of their five children became ill with a fever. In 1966 Jeffrey Moses tried to buy the lighthouse. He had spent many summer holidays at Talacre as a boy and fallen in love with the place. Immediately after he made an offer to purchase the tower he fell ill, unexpectedly, and died a short while later. He was thirty-eight years old.

On 22 April 2006 a team of eight paranormal investigators, using modern techniques examined Talacre lighthouse, searching for evidence that would explain the sightings. They set up night vision cameras on every floor and placed motion sensors, sound detectors, electromagnetic sensors and digital cameras throughout the lighthouse. During the night they heard strange sounds and their monitors went crazy. While this was going on, Mary White, a respected medium, was conducting a séance during which she made contact with four spirits. One of the spirits told her he was Raymond, a lighthouse keeper who had died of fever, possibly typhoid, and a broken heart.

One medium claimed that the spirit of one of the lighthouse keepers has returned to his duties and that his name is either Daniel or Samuel. No record exists of a keeper at Talacre named Daniel. Has the ghost of Samuel Brooks, the lighthouse keeper who lived there with his wife until 1844, come back? We can speculate but no one really knows.

Today, if you visit Talacre beach and look up at the lighthouse you will see the figure of a man near the lantern but it isn't the ghost of the lighthouse keeper, Raymond or any other spectre. The 7 foot tall figure is a sculpture, named 'The Keeper' that was placed on the balcony of the lighthouse in 2010. Said to represent the ghost, the artwork is made of 120 pieces of stainless steel designed to let the wind blow through it and, according to the artist, make an unsettling moaning noise.

10

Dry Bridge Lodge
Holywell

Strangers travelling along a minor road south-west of Mostyn (near Holywell/*Treffynnon*) are surprised to find themselves driving under a house. The structure, known as Dry Bridge Lodge, was designed and built in 1849 by the Architect Ambrose Poynter, on the instructions of Edward Pryce Lloyd, 1st Baron Mostyn. The baron was a politician and, at different times, the High Sheriff of Flintshire, Caernarfonshire and Meirionnydd.

Mostyn Hall, the Baron's country seat, had been the ancestral home since the fifteenth century. The Mostyns originated from Pengwern, Llangollen, in the fourteenth century, and over successive years a succession of strategic marriages made them a very powerful family. In the nineteenth century, the Mostyns were the biggest landowners in north Wales. An 1883 return shows their estates covered 7,779 acres. When, in 1848 Owen Williams, a Liverpool architect, produced plans to build a holiday resort on salt marshes near Great Orme, the Baron was enthusiastic. Mostyn Estates owned the land and he immediately saw the potential of the idea. Victorian engineers were constructing a railway line from Crewe to Holyhead (*Caergybi*), passing along the north Wales coast, and it would bring visitors. A small

Dry Bridge Lodge, viewed from the road, built for Lord Mostyn's convenience when visiting Whitford

Dry Bridge Lodge showing the carriageway arch

community already existed at Llandudno, housing workers in the Great Orme (*Gogarth*) copper mines and a few fishermen, but it was struggling because the copper mines were almost worked out. They closed in 1850.

Baron Mostyn expanded the architect's plans to cover 995 acres and kept tight control of what could be built. He wanted a holiday resort that was attractive as well as practical, and appointed the architect George Felton to oversee all aspects of the development. A new branch line was constructed, linking Llandudno to the express train line. It opened in 1858. Prime land was leased to hoteliers and other businessmen, wanting to be involved, and the new resort grew quickly.

While Llandudno was being built, Baron Mostyn was also engaged in rebuilding his home, Mostyn Hall. The hall was extended in a Jacobean style and the park enlarged southwards, towards the village of Whitford. The baron wanted a new carriageway laid between the Hall and Whitford (*Chwitffordd*) but to do so it had to cross a public road. His architect Poynter knew that, to please the baron, the drive needed to be private, and he came up with an ingenious solution: lower the road and build a bridge over it to carry the carriageway, but he didn't stop there. Poynter constructed a gatehouse on top of the bridge.

The resulting house, known as Dry Bridge Lodge, was finished in 1849. Viewed from the road it is a narrow two-storey house with battlements balanced on the bridge but, seen from the carriageway, Dry Bridge Lodge is a substantial double-fronted gatehouse with an archway, and a tunnel passing through its centre.

Baron Mostyn's holiday town was a success and became a popular Victorian holiday destination. In 1864, Llandudno was named 'Queen of the Welsh Resorts'. One famous visitor was Queen Elizabeth of Romania. She stayed for five weeks and described the town as 'a beautiful haven of peace', which translates as, '*Hardd, hafan, hedd*'. Following the queen's visit, the Welsh translation was adopted as the town's official motto.

Today, Llandudno is the largest seaside holiday resort in Wales, much of it still owned by Mostyn Estates. The town is a Victorian time capsule and many of the buildings have been listed as architecturally important. Dry Bridge Lodge was made a Grade II* listed building in October 1969. The listing text describes the lodge as 'One of a fine series of nineteenth-century lodges and gates forming the architectural setting of Mostyn Park.' The lodge is still occupied but carriages no longer travel along the driveway and the gates are kept firmly closed.

11

Mynydd y Garreg Tower
Whitford

It is said that there have been towers on Mynydd y Garreg (*mynydd*: mountain; *carreg*: stone) in Flintshire since Roman times. If true, the first was probably a Pharos tower which, like the magnificent Pharos of Alexandria, was built to guide sailors safely into port. During the day, mirrors on Alexandria's Pharos reflected the sun's rays out to sea and at night a beacon fire blazed at the top of the tower. The Egyptian Pharos was believed to be 450 feet (140 metres) tall and regarded as one of the seven wonders of the ancient world. A beacon fire may have been lit on the Garreg pharos but the tower would have been much smaller than its Egyptian namesake. The Roman garrison at Deva Victrix (Chester; *Caer*) required regular resupply. Deva Victrix was a provincial capital and one of the biggest Roman fortresses, leading historians to speculate that it was the capital of Britannia. The amphitheatre at Deva Victrix could seat more than 8,000 spectators and was the largest in Britain. The easiest way to transport supplies, needed to maintain so many people, was by sea. Roman mariners used the Pharos to navigate safely into the Dee before completing the final part of their voyage, a 20-mile journey upstream to the fortress.

Mynydd Garreg Tower still guards the Dee Estuary

At the end of the fourth century, after more than 300 years of occupation, the Roman legions withdrew from Britain, Diva Victrix was evacuated and the Pharos on Mynydd y Garreg was abandoned.

With the disappearance of Roman imperial authority, and the legions who imposed it, Roman 'law and order' broke down, giving way to the indigenous culture of the previously colonised, now liberated, people. Without empire, culture became more varied and localised, and trade diminished. Literacy survived in high Irish culture and high Welsh culture, with the evolution of Celtic Christianity. However, because of the paucity of Latin or Greek written histories, this time was later, incorrectly, called 'The Dark Ages'.

With the Roman legions gone, populations began to move. The Viking outlaws raided the coasts of Wales, mainly plundering the high art (gold) in Welsh monasteries. Viking outlaws were succeeded by Viking settlers. Coastal villagers built watchtowers to warn of approaching ships, and the Pharos tower was found a new purpose, as a lookout point where sentries stood, ready to raise the alarm.

More than a thousand years passed until, in the fifteenth century, the threat from seaborne cut-throats had reduced. Watchtowers fell into disuse and stood empty, but not for very long. Maintaining law and order was expensive and, to raise the money needed new taxes, which are never popular, were introduced. Because of the taxes, salt and other essentials were more expensive in the land than abroad and smugglers began to profit from the differences in price. Lookout towers became observation points for the king's revenue men to watch for ships smuggling contraband. Salt coming from Ireland was a particular problem and the tower on Mynydd y Garreg was ideal for guarding the Dee estuary. Ironically, much of the salt being smuggled originated from Cheshire. Eventually the salt tax was abolished and the tower fell into disuse once again.

On 20 June 1897, Queen Victoria had reigned for sixty years and subjects across the kingdom were celebrating her diamond jubilee. To honour the queen's anniversary, Llewelyn Nevill Vaughan Lloyd-Mostyn, 3rd Baron Mostyn of Flintshire, rebuilt the derelict tower on Mynydd y Garreg. The modest structure he erected, which stands on the site today, is a circular stone tower with a doorway, window openings and mock battlements.

British Listed Buildings made Mynydd y Garreg tower a Grade II listed building in 1952. The tower is a distance from the road but the views from the top of the mountain justify the walk.

12

The Hallelujah Obelisk
Mold

In 1736, landowner Nehemiah Griffiths, who lived at Rhual, Mold (*Yr Wuddgrug*), built an obelisk in one of his fields. The stone monument he erected included a Latin inscription and was built to commemorate one of the strangest battles having been recorded as taking place in Wales. But why did a farmer, with nothing to gain, suddenly decide to erect a rather sad and forlorn looking structure in the corner of one of his fields? To understand this we need to go back nearly 1,300 years. For centuries there had been stories that a battle had been fought in the area. Bede, an ancient chronicler, had told of a great battle. There were reports of a ghostly giant warrior wearing a golden cloak being seen on a nearby mound known as Goblin Hill (*Bryn yr Ellyllon*). The spectre would beckon onlookers to come closer and locals, fearful of the apparition, learned to avoid the area.

In 1833, nearly 100 years after the obelisk was built, Goblin Hill was excavated and revealed to be a burial cairn. Within the cairn, a skeleton was discovered wearing a magnificent golden cape. The cape had been made from a single ingot of gold weighing more than ½ kg (1.1 lb) which had been hammered until it was a thin sheet of gold foil and then embossed with intricate patterns to make it look

Hallelujah Obelisk,
built to celebrate
an historic victory

like a beautiful folded cloth. Because the cape was so delicate, it broke up as it was removed from the grave. Workmen plundered pieces of the cape before what remained was sent to the British Museum. The museum identified the garment as having been made during the Bronze Age, over 1600 years before Christ was born and stated 'that it was one of the finest examples of prehistoric sheet-gold working and unique in form and design'.

Who was the ghostly warrior buried with such a fine garment? One possible explanation is that he was killed during a battle that took place nearby. According to Leigh's *Guide to Wales and Monmouthshire*, published in 1835, a ferocious battle, known as '*Victoria Alleluiatica*', had been fought between a Christian Welsh force and an invading army of Picts and Saxons. Different versions of the story date the battle between AD 429 and 448. By then, the Romans had withdrawn from Britain, leaving the islands undefended and vulnerable to invasion. Hordes of Picts from Scotland and Friesians, Angles and Saxons from Germanic lands drove the Celtic population west as they advanced across the land.

A small Christian army led by Bishop Germanus chose to stand and fight near what is now the town of Mold in Flintshire. The Welsh defenders were heavily outnumbered and defeat looked inevitable. As the bishop marshalled his men in preparation for the coming fight, he tried to think of a way to inspire them. He needed a battle cry to embolden his army and strike fear into the hearts of the approaching heathens.

By now, the invading pagans were close at hand. Suddenly, an ancient Hebrew word sprang to mind and Bishop Germanus ordered his men to shout it as loudly as they could. 'Hallel-ujah', screamed the men and again they cried, 'Hallel-ujah'. Three times in all they shouted 'Hallel-ujah', which means, 'Praise Jehovah' or 'Praise the Lord' (the normal Christian interpretation of the words). Hearing the strange battle cry, the pagan invaders were confused. Some turned and ran north, only to be driven into the river Alyn, where they drowned. Others were struck down by the swords of the triumphant Welshmen. It was a great victory which secured the land of Wales for the Celtic race.

The identity of the warrior with the golden cloak, or which side he was on, has never been established and will probably remain a mystery. Indeed, there is no evidence to prove he was even on the battlefield that day. Considering that the golden cloak he was buried with would have been 2000 years old at the time of the battle his presence is rather unlikely and his burial nearby probably nothing more than a coincidence.

There is another Hebrew meaning of '*Hallel*': someone that acts madly or foolishly. It would have been a truthful description of Germanus' outnumbered army's position. If Germanus had cried '*Hallel!*' it would have been a bit like the character Frazer in *Dad's Army*, who cries out, 'We're doomed ...'. The morale of the army would have been destroyed. The outcome of the battle known as '*Victoria Alleluiatica*', and the future of the Celtic nation that is Wales, would have been very different.

13

Tŷ Castell
Mold

The Elizabethan country house, Nercwys Hall near Mold, was built by John Wynn in the 1638. Wynn, a wealthy gentleman, left the estate to his son Robert and there followed a succession of inheritances through the female line until, in 1765, it was owned by John Giffard. The Giffard family were staunch Catholics and recusants. The Recusancy Act, passed in 1593 during Elizabeth I's reign, made it an offence to refuse to attend Anglican Church services. The Act, described as 'An act for restraining Popish recusants,' prescribed civil and criminal punishments including fines, imprisonment and, in extreme case, execution. Other religious groups were also targeted as recusants, including dissenting Protestants and Calvinists. Notable recusants of the time included Guy Fawkes and William Shakespeare, who came from a Catholic recusant family.

John Giffard died in 1797 and Nercwys Hall passed to his daughter, Elizabeth Giffard. Elizabeth, a spinster, added large Gothic wings to the hall. One commentator, clearly not impressed, described them as 'elephantine'. Other alterations followed, including a new gatehouse, a garden with battlement walls, an orangery and a stove house. In 1825 she built 'Tŷ Castell,'a folly north of the hall. Built in the same style

Tŷ Castell, once a rather majestic cow shed

as the new wings, the folly was visually complete when viewed from the hall, but was a two dimensional Gothic façade with nothing much behind. The folly, built at the highest point in the park, was designed to be enjoyed from the hall. When Elizabeth died in 1842, aged seventy-six, she bequeathed Nercwys Hall to Reverend Maurice Wynn, thus ending eighty years of Catholic ownership.

Elizabeth I's original recusancy laws were repealed in 1650. By then, a number of Catholics had become martyrs, many convicted in show trials. In 1970, Pope Paul VI canonized forty of them including six

Welshmen. The Welsh Catholic Church commemorates them with a feast day on 25 October. Many restrictions on the Roman Catholic faith continued until 1829 and the introduction of the Catholic Relief Act. But it was not until 2013 that an Act of Parliament was introduced to repeal the ancient laws disqualifying Catholics from the throne. The same Act ends male primacy and allows daughters to rank above their younger brothers in the line to the throne.

In the 1960s, the Gothic wings and porch from Nercwys Hall were dismantled. The porch was later salvaged and rebuilt at Portmeirion by Sir Clough Williams-Ellis. The folly became a Grade II listed building in 1952 and was restored in 1970. The Royal Commission of the Ancient and Historical Monuments of Wales describes Tŷ Castell as a cowshed. At one time there was, it seems, a lean-to building behind the folly used to accommodate cattle. It's difficult to imagine a cowshed with a more regal facade.

14

Chirk Castle Gates

Visitors to Chirk Castle are impressed. The National Trust, who maintain the castle and open it to the public, provide tours and the guides are well versed in its history. The formal gardens are a delight and the park with its views of the castle, hidden forest paths and statues are a pleasure to stroll through. As you drive away from the castle you are taken along a one-way system that returns you to the public road where a strange, some say beautiful, set of gates have been erected. The position of the gates seems out of place. The gates rarely open and the road is diverted around them. Most people, satisfied that their visit is over, drive past the gates without appreciating them, but it's worth stopping to fully enjoy the workmanship of this wonderful folly.

The Myddelton family had been prominent in welsh affairs since the fifteenth century and were founder members of the East India Company, which financed the voyages of Drake, Raleigh and Hawkins, raiding Spanish colonies and shipping for treasure. Thomas Myddelton, who had once been an apprentice grocer, gambled everything on the venture. The privateers returned with their ships loaded with gold, silver and jewels making Thomas Myddelton wealthy. In 1595 he bought Chirk Castle for £5,000, entered parliament, purchased estates in Essex and bought

Chirk Castle Gates

various lordships including a baronetcy.

During the Civil War his son, also a Thomas, was a parliamentary commander who helped defeat the royalists, sending Charles I to his death. During the war, Chirk Castle was captured by royalist forces and held for three years. Thomas Myddelton was reluctant to attack his own home and bribed the royalists to leave. Having done so he, perhaps foolishly, changed sides and a parliamentary army bombarded the castle causing considerable damage. Despite fighting for both sides, the Myddeltons survived the restoration of the monarchy and felt secure enough to begin a major rebuilding of Chirk Castle. It was completed in 1672. Improvements to the castle continued with each generation adding something new. In 1711 it was Sir

Richard Myddelton's turn. He commissioned Robert and John Davies, brothers who were blacksmiths in Wrexham, to make a set of wrought iron gates for the castle.

The Davies brothers were highly skilled artisans and Sir Richard was obliged to pay them the princely sum of two shillings (10p) a day for their labour. Sir Richard, it was agreed, would provide the wrought iron needed to construct the gates. Sir Richard wanted the gates to tell the story of the Myddeltons and instructed the blacksmiths to include features describing the family. One was a red hand alluding to a legendary dispute between two Myddelton brothers over who should inherit the castle. They agreed to settle the matter by a running race with the winner, the one to touch the gates first with his hand, getting the castle. Presumably there were other castle gates at the time of the race. The brothers ran neck and neck and one was about to win when the second brother drew his sword and cut off the outstretched hand.

Sir Richard waited eight years, far longer than he expected, to see the new gates he had ordered but was pleased with the result. The gates the Davies brothers created were huge pieces of baroque art, incorporating wolves' heads, eagles and acanthus scrolls. The arch above the gates included the Myddelton coat of arms and the bloody red hand. Whether Sir Richard expected such big gates isn't recorded, but having agreed a day rate for the job, no one could blame the blacksmiths for stretching the work out for as long as possible. Sir Richard had planned to site the gates on the main drive to the castle but they were so overwhelming he changed his mind and had them set up to form a courtyard at the side of the castle.

In 1771 another Myddelton, who was possibly less impressed with the gigantic wrought iron gates, had them removed to a different site on the estate. In 1888, the gates, which by now were looking shabby, were moved for a third time to their present location, out of sight of the castle. Since then the gates have been restored to their original glory and are magnificent examples of eighteenth-century wrought iron workmanship.

The Royal Commission of Ancient and Historic Monuments has listed the gates and describes them thus, 'Cast and wrought ironwork, painted black with gold highlights. Piers with Corinthian capitals; vine tendrils and coronets to central openwork shaft; lead wolf finials; Twin carriage gates with scrolled foliage; heraldic overthrow containing the Myddleton (*sic*) arms. Spear finials and scrollwork cresting to side gates and railing. Square stone piers, with pineapple finials.' What more can one say?

15

The Acton Screen
Wrexham

Drive north along Chester Road in Wrexham (*Wrecsam*) and you will pass an incongruous structure on your right comprising pillars, metal railings and a gateway. Sitting on the top of the structure are four white greyhounds, and immediately behind sits a modest housing estate, which is clearly from a different, more modern, period. Known as the Acton Screen, the structure was the entrance to a driveway that led to Acton Hall. The hall, once part of a prominent estate, has been demolished, leaving the proud entrance screen standing alone and looking out of place in its modern setting.

The screen was built in about 1810 by the then owner, Sir Foster Cunliffe. He had a passion for greyhounds and included four wooden dogs on the top of the screen. In 1917 Sir Bernard Oppenheimer, the diamond merchant, purchased Acton Hall and opened it as a school to teach disabled ex-servicemen how to cut and polish diamonds. Oppenheimer tried to relocate the dogs to his own home but was persuaded to leave them on the screen when he realised they were made of wood. During the Second World War the Hall was requisitioned by the authorities and, in 1943, the US Army moved in. When they left, Acton Hall was in a poor state of

Acton Park Screen,
all that remains of the hanging judge's home

repair and, it has been alleged, one of the dogs had vanished; taken by the Americans as a souvenir. The current dogs were mounted on the screen in 1982 and are made of fibreglass.

Acton Hall was also the home of the Jeffreys family; its most notorious resident was George Jeffreys, 1st Baron Jeffrey of Wem. George was born at Acton in 1645 and went on to become a judge. He wasn't a popular man and had few friends. King Charles II commented, 'He has no learning, no sense, no manners and has more impudence than ten streetwalkers'.

Charles II had no legitimate offspring and his younger brother James was next in line for the crown.

James had spent part of his life in France and secretly converted to Catholicism, although he still attended Anglican services. This, and his marriage to an Italian Catholic princess, made him an unpopular figure and attempts were made to have him excluded from the line of accession. When, in 1678, an apparent Catholic plot to kill Charles II was uncovered, Judge Jeffreys sent more than twenty-two men to the gallows. Many of them were later found to have been innocent. Innocence or guilt didn't concern Judge Jeffreys in the least and, having just sentenced men to death on the flimsiest of pretexts, he would spend his time drinking and carousing. Commentators described him as an alcoholic, vengeful man with a violent temper. Despite his lack of social graces and disrespect for the law, Jeffreys became Chief Justice of Chester in 1680 and went on to serve as Lord Chief Justice of England.

When Charles II' brother James was implicated in the plot, Members of Parliament proposed that the crown should pass instead to James Scott, 1st Duke of Monmouth. Hearing of the attempt to usurp his brother, Charles dissolved Parliament.

Following the death of Charles II, in 1685, the crown passed to his brother, who became King James II. At the same time the Duke of Monmouth led a rebellion and attempted to seize the crown for himself. The duke was the illegitimate son of Charles II. Although Monmouth had been recognised as the king's son and given a dukedom, he had no legal right to the throne. Despite this, he printed leaflets proclaiming himself king and raised an army. James

II responded and defeated Monmouth on 6 July 1685 at the Battle of Sedgemoor. It was the last pitched battle to take place in the British Isles. Monmouth was captured and beheaded at Tower Hill. Accounts record that it took five axe blows to cut off his head.

Legend has it that, following Monmouth's execution, it was realised that there was no official portrait of him. To remedy this, his body was exhumed, the head stitched back on and a portrait painted of the lifeless corpse. Another rumour was that James II, not wanting to execute his nephew, arranged for some other unfortunate fellow to take his place on the scaffold and sent the dishonoured Monmouth to the King of France where he became the 'Man in the Iron Mask.'

Such mercy was not shown to other conspirators; it was now that Judge Jeffreys, with his cavalier attitude to justice, made his name. In the autumn of 1865 the Judge travelled to Taunton in Somerset where most of the traitors were tried. Since the plot had been attempting to remove a Catholic king, and Jeffreys' contempt for Catholics was well known, some defendants were expecting leniency. They were disappointed. On 18 and 19 September alone, he condemned 144 people to death. The trial became known as the 'Bloody Assizes', and Judge Jeffreys earned himself the nickname 'The Hanging Judge'. Reports from the trial allege that Judge Jeffreys taunted defendants, extorted money from their families with promises of leniency, and then sent them to the gallows. It's estimated that, during the trial, he sentenced 300 to death and between 800 and 900 to be transported to the West Indies as slaves.

Because of his terrible treatment of innocent men, Jeffreys became a figure of scorn and hate. The resentment of Catholics, and King James in particular continued despite the king's liberal approach to all religions. There was a second Protestant rebellion when, in 1688, parliament offered the throne to William of Orange and his wife Mary. Mary was James II's daughter but, like her husband, was Protestant. William was proclaimed King William III and ruled jointly with his wife. James fled to France and exile after, it is said, throwing his seal of office into the Thames. Following his escape, Parliament passed a law to exclude any future Catholic from ascending the throne. One of the reasons cited for this law was the cruel punishments handed out by the king's judges.

Without King James' support, Judge Jeffreys had no protection, and fearful for his own safety, decided to follow James to France. To avoid vengeful citizens, he disguised himself as a sailor and made his way to Wapping intending to make his escape. Unfortunately for him, the judge made the mistake of visiting a tavern where he was recognised, chased by a mob and caught. A search of his baggage revealed 35,000 guineas and a large hoard of silver, suggesting that he was trying to flee with the money stolen from his victims.

Judge Jeffreys begged the authorities to protect him from the mob and, for his own protection, was taken to the Tower of London where he remained for four months. He was never convicted of any crime, and died in the Tower from natural causes on 18 April 1689. Not surprisingly, there isn't a monument to the judge in his home town.

Acton Hall was demolished in 1854 but the Acton Screen, which is all that remains, serves as a reminder of one of the most odious judges in British history.

16

Clocaenog Forest Memorial
Denbighshire

The Bagot family has a long and proud ancestry. According to research published in 1824 by William Bagot, the 2nd Baron Bagot, his family's roots can be traced to a time before the Norman invasion in 1066. The family seat was in Staffordshire but, over time, they added estates in Kent and Denbighshire. One of these was Pool Park, which Sir Walter Bagot acquired by marriage in the early 1700s. The Bagot family had already obtained, as part of an earlier dowry, the nearby Bachymbyd Estate, but Pool Park would become the family's main residence in Wales. Altogether the family owned 18,000 acres in Denbighshire. This, together with revenues from their other estates, produced a substantial income.

In 1828, the country house at Pool Park was rebuilt in the style of an Elizabethan mansion. As well as building a new home and spending time researching his family history, Baron Bagot took an active interest in his estates, funding almshouses and other projects to improve the lives of his tenants. One improvement involved planting an area of woodland which would become known as Clocaenog Forest. As the woodland was created, the baron added a large stone obelisk on the site of an ancient cairn.

The Bagot family continued to own Pool Park until

Clocaenog Forest Monument
celebrating one of the first conservationists

their estates in Denbighshire were sold in 1928. Pool Park passed into the possession of the Tate family, of Tate and Lyle sugar. In 1937 the mansion changed hands again and opened as a mental asylum for eighty-seven long-stay patients. It closed in the 1990s. Since then the building has been unoccupied. A plan to redevelop the hall to use it as a nursing home, submitted in 2012, was recently rejected by the local authority. The once elegant house remains vacant and is now blighted by decay and vandalism.

Clocaenog Forest was eventually taken over by the Forestry Commission, who expanded it with a major planting campaign in 1905. Today, Clocaenog Forest extends to 40 square miles (100 square kms). It is the biggest Welsh refuge for native red squirrels and a home to some rare Przewalski's Horses, purchased by the Forestry Commission from the Welsh Mountain Zoo in 2003 to graze a 12-acre paddock.

The forest is a popular place for walkers and cyclists with easy access, good paths and various points of interest including a stone circle and ancient sites of worship. One track in the forest is referred to as Lady Bagot's Drive because, apparently, it was used by the baron and his wife for carriage rides.

Not all visitors, however, go to Clocaenog to enjoy themselves. In 2002, a schizophrenic by the name of Richard Sumner handcuffed himself to a tree in a remote part of the forest and threw the key away. It was three years before a woman walking her dog discovered his skeleton. Damage to the tree suggested that the unfortunate man had a change of heart and tried to break free before he died.

The Clocaenog Forest Memorial, sometimes called the Bagot Memorial, was registered as a Grade II listed structure in December 2001. Without it there would be little to remind anyone of William Bagot, the man who planted a forest and created an amenity which, 200 years later, we can all enjoy. It's an impressive monument in a prominent position and those who climb up from the car park to see it will be rewarded by superb views of Snowdonia in the west, the Berwyn Mountains (*Mynydd y Berwyn*) lying south and the Clwydian Range (*Bryniau Clwyd*) to the east.

17

Nantclwyd Rotunda
Rhuthun

Nantclwyd Hall is a seventeenth-century country house, near Rhuthun, belonging to Sir Philip Vyvyan Naylor-Leyland, the 4th Baronet. His ancestor, Sir Herbert Scarisbrick Naylor-Leyland, was a Conservative politician and Member of Parliament. Sir Herbert's mother had been a Scarisbrick and his father a Naylor-Leyland. Both were wealthy families. In 1873, while staying at Nanclwyd Hall, Major Walter Wingfield entertained other house guests with a game using a rubber ball and a racket. The major started to market his new game in 1874 and patented 'an improved court for playing the ancient game of tennis'. The rules and scoring invented by Wingfield are the basis of modern lawn tennis.

Sir Herbert and his attractive wife, an American heiress, moved in the same circles as the future Edward VII, who became the godfather of Albert, their first son, who was born in 1890.

Another son, George, had the Duke of York, later King George V, as his godfather. According to local legend, Sir Herbert built a railway station for Queen Victoria to use during a brief visit. It was later demolished and the track ripped up.

In 1895, aged thirty-two, Sir Herbert was made a baronet by the Earl of Rosebury. Following his sudden

Nantclwyd Rotunda, where lawn tennis was invented

and unexpected elevation to the peerage, he resigned from the Conservative party and joined the Liberals, voting with them on important legislation – in return, according to some, for the peerage. At the time, Lord Rosebury, a Liberal parliamentarian married to Hannah de Rothschild, was Prime Minister.

Sir Herbert died from a throat infection aged thirty-five.

During the twentieth century, the family decided to improve the landscape at Nantclwyd and commissioned the architect Sir Clough Williams-Ellis to undertake the structural elements of the project. The design included an Italian garden, a park, a lake, temples and follies including a rotunda. The rotunda stands beside the lake in the park north of the hall, and was completed in 1965.

Cadw's 2001 listing for the rotunda described it as:

an octagonal rotunda on Tuscan columns, with a domed roof crowned by a gilded globe emerging from petals. Stylobate – a reference to the style of plinth – with three concrete steps. The soffit is a flat ceiling painted with the signs of the zodiac.

Nantclwyd Hall and its gardens remain private (although the gardens were opened to the public in 2003 as part of the National Gardens Scheme) but it is still possible to view the rotunda. A public footpath crosses the park, passing the rotunda, where hikers can enjoy its simple beauty, framed exquisitely with a background of the lake and the great house beyond.

18

Moel Fama's Egyptian Temple
Rhuthun

Sitting high on a ridge on the Clwydian Mountains, between Flintshire and Denbighshire, the tower on Moel Fama is a dominant feature and can be seen for miles in all directions. Today, the structure looks imposing – but what you see is only a small part of what was originally planned. The tower was designed to be a monumental building celebrating the longest-reigning British monarch there had ever been.

King George III, the first Hanoverian king of Britain to speak English as his main language, had been on the throne for nearly forty years. Unlike his German father, he was born in Britain and had never visited Hanover. Some called him 'mad George' because he suffered periods of mental illness. It wasn't his only nickname. When his government levied taxes on tea and newspapers, in the American Colonies to help pay for the French Indian war, they took exception and rebelled. Following a bloody war, America gained its independence. 'Mad King George has lost us America', cried the people. Unkind commentators called him Farmer George because he preferred gardening and growing vegetables to matters of state. But, as George got older, the people grew to admire him for his piety and modesty.

'We must do something to celebrate the king's

Moel Famau, a monument to a king that was never completed

golden jubilee!' announced the splendidly named Reverend Whitehall-Whitehall Davies. The reverend, a local squire, wrote to his friend Lord Kenyon and they formed a committee to decide what to do.

'Let's erect a giant tower,' they said and sent for a famous architect. The architect, Thomas Harrison, got to work and produced a design for a 115-foot tower resembling an Egyptian temple.

'We need to put the tower somewhere high, so it can be seen from miles away. Moel Fama would be perfect,' suggested the Reverend. The committee agreed. Moel Fama is the highest hill in the Clwydian Range, making the planned monument visible for miles.

On 24 October 1810, the year of the king's jubilee,

Lord Kenyon laid the foundation stone. Special sermons, to commemorate the event, were preached in Mold and Ruthin. Then, dignitaries rode horses to the top of Moel Fama, accompanied by a band of musicians and beautiful female attendants. More than 5000 people climbed to the top of Moel Fama to witness the great occasion. Pits were dug and filled with wood to roast oxen and '*cwrw da*' – 'good beer' was served to aid the day long festivities.

Following the laying of the foundation stone, things began to go wrong. The Wrexham surveyor Thomas Penson had calculated the cost of building the tower to be £3235. A public fund had been started to pay for the work but only raised £1129. The people of Denbighshire and Flintshire loved their king but not quite enough to pay for such an extravagant monument. Lord Kenyon added £650 to bolster the fund and building work began. From the start, there were problems. Lack of money and constant bickering between the architect and the surveyor resulted in the project slowing to a snail's pace. By 1815, Penson and Harrison were no longer cooperating and it became clear the original design was unaffordable. Things dragged on until, in 1817, a more modest and less costly design was agreed. Construction progressed until the money ran out and work ceased on the half-finished jubilee tower.

The monument remained as it was for the next twenty-nine years. The residents of Denbighshire and Flintshire had lost interest in their celebratory jubilee tower. In 1846, one corner of the tower collapsed.

Poorly constructed foundations and shoddy workmanship had left the structure unsafe and needing urgent repairs. A new fund was started and, with the £500 it raised, limited repairs could be made to the tower.

In October 1862, following two days of storms, the half-built jubilee tower collapsed. All that remained was the plinth and a pile of rubble. Local people pilfered material to build stone walls and the remains of the tower became an eyesore visible for miles.

King George III died in 1820, after almost sixty years on the throne. By then he was blind and deaf, and had what we now know as dementia. He was, at the time, the longest-reigning British monarch. Later monarchs Victoria and Elizabeth II would reign longer. In 1970 the site of the jubilee tower was tidied up to look as it does today and it is now part of a country park. From a distance, the plinth, all that remains of the tower, looks more like a mausoleum than the base of an Egyptian tower, built to celebrate the reign of mad King George, who lost America.

19

Folly Castle, Plas Brondanw
Carreg Llanfrothen

Plas Brondanw is a picturesque estate in Carreg Llanfrothen, Snowdonia (*Eryri*). In 1908 the estate was inherited by a 25-year-old architect, Clough Williams-Ellis. Although Williams-Ellis was born in England, his family came from Welsh stock and he claimed to be a direct descendant of Owain Gwynedd, a twentieth-century Welsh prince. He was educated at Oundle School, Northamptonshire and went on to study at Cambridge, but never graduated from the University. After leaving Cambridge he spent a few months studying architecture, followed by a brief period working for an architectural firm before setting up his own practice.

In 1908 William-Ellis' father died and he inherited the family home, Plas Brondanw, where he built his first folly, known as Folly Castle.

His legacy was in a run-down condition and Williams-Ellis enthusiastically began the job of restoring the house and gardens to their former glory. The house he inherited had been converted into flats and the gardens divided to make allotments. Restoring Plas Brondanw became a long project that Williams-Ellis continued for much of his life.

During World War One, Williams-Ellis served with the Welsh Guards and won a Military Cross. In 1915

Folly Castle, a present to Sir Clough Williams-Ellis from his comrades in arms

he became engaged to the writer Amabel Strachey. When his commanding officer asked what the other officers should buy Williams-Ellis and his bride as a wedding present he replied, 'Well, sir, what I would really like is a ruin.'

According to Williams-Ellis, the answer bemused the CO, who had previously suggested that a silver salver would be a most suitable gift. Ellis explained there was a rocky eminence near his home that was ideal for a lookout tower to view Snowdon (*Yr Wyddfa*). 'Well, if you want a ruin, I suppose you had better have a ruin – though it's an odd sort of wedding present, I must say,' agreed the CO, and the matter was settled.

The ruin that Williams-Ellis built on his rocky

eminence was named 'Folly Castle'. It included a three-storey tower, ruined wall and battlements finished in a Welsh medieval style. A plaque above the entrance states:

> This outlook tower was subscribed for as a wedding present to Clough Williams-Ellis and his bride Amabel Strachey in 1915 by his brother officers of the Welsh Guards. In the Second World War it was prepared as a local military strongpoint to repel the expected German invasion.

After the First World War, Clough Williams-Ellis continued practising as an architect and in 1920 began work on his pet project, the Italianate village, Portmeirion, which made him famous. The house at Plas Brondanw was seriously damaged by fire in 1951 and Williams-Ellis undertook a major reconstruction of the property. A flaming urn statue at the top of a waterfall in the garden commemorates the fire.

Today ownership of the Plas Brondanw Estate has been passed from the Williams-Ellis family to a charitable trust, and the gardens, including Folly Castle, are open to the public. Clough Williams-Ellis was knighted in 1972 'for services to the preservation of the environment and to architecture', and was the oldest person to have received the honour. He continued working into his nineties and died aged ninety-four. The mock castle at Plas Brondanw may have been the earliest of his follies but more extraordinary and beautiful buildings followed, making Sir Clough Williams-Ellis the most prolific folly-builder in Wales.

20

Portmeirion
Minffordd, Porthmadog

The holiday village of Portmeirion, near Porthmadog, is one of Wales' most popular tourist attractions. Sir Clough Williams-Ellis of Plas Brondanw built the village in an eclectic Mediterranean style.

After serving in the Second World War Clough's architectural practice prospered and he designed many notable buildings. As well as taking design commissions in his business, in 1925 Williams-Ellis began work on what would become his most enduring creation: Portmeirion. While certainly not a 'folly', it could be said to be a remarkable and beautiful 'curiosity'.

His new village incorporated a medieval castle, boatyard, an eighteenth-century foundry and buildings, which formed part of an estate known as 'Aber Iâ'. Williams-Ellis disliked the name and, having bought the estate, changed it to Portmeirion, to indicate that the village was by the sea and in the county of Meirionnydd. One of the first buildings to be completed was the Portmeirion Hotel, which opened in 1926.

More buildings followed and, as they did, Williams-Ellis' vision of a continental town complete with plazas and swaying palm trees was revealed. Taking ideas from across the world, and willing to

Portmeirion, a cornucopia of follies

include parts from demolished buildings, he mixed Burmese statues with Greek gods, Corinthian columns with modest bungalows and created a magical vista of symmetry, illusion and interest. As well as looking attractive, many of the buildings were designed to be functional; some are now holiday cottages. Many famous people visited: for example, in 1941 Noel Coward wrote his play *Blithe Spirit* in one of the suites in the hotel.

Because of its stunning beauty, Portmeirion has been used as a film and television set for a variety of productions, most notable of which was the 1960s cult television series *The Prisoner*, starring Patrick McGoohan.

In addition to developing Portmeirion, Williams-Ellis was a prime mover in the creation of the Snowdonia National Park (*Parc Cenedlaethol Eryri*). He ran a long campaign to preserve Snowdonia and donated 300 acres of land, towards the creation of the park. In 1972 he was knighted for 'services to architecture and the environment', the oldest person ever to be knighted, aged eighty-eight years.

The biggest building on the Aber Iâ Estate had been Castell Deudraeth and Williams-Ellis planned to use the building as part of a hotel complex. Sadly, he never saw it completed. Sir Clough Williams-Ellis died aged ninetey-four, in April 1978. Following his death, his body was cremated and, according to his instructions, the ashes were incorporated in a large rocket, later used during a New Year's Eve fireworks display at Portmeirion.

Although William-Ellis is no longer alive, his legacy continues to grow. Castell Deudraeth was completed and opened as a hotel in 2001. Today, Portmeirion is administered by a charitable trust, used as a holiday complex, is a popular venue for weddings, and the home of a variety of music festivals, including Festival No6 – the name referring back to *The Prisoner*.

21

The Bryncir Tower
Cricieth

The family of Joseph Huddart, a Cumberland man born in 1741, wanted him to become a priest but he rebelled and ran away to sea. Huddart worked as a fisherman, catching the herring which were abundant in the Firth of Forth at that time. Hearing of the vast shoals of herring being caught and the potential profits, his father relented and invested in curing houses where the fish could be smoked. The business prospered, but in 1762 Huddart's father suddenly died, whereupon the young man joined the East India Company and sailed for India. By 1778, while still a relatively young man, Huddart had reached the rank of Naval Commander and was comfortably wealthy.

Joseph Huddart gained a reputation as a skilled cartographer and navigator and was a highly respected company man. Ten years later, in 1788, he retired to enjoy the wealth that he had accumulated. Now, with time on his hands, Huddart turned his attention to science and its practical application of machines. In 1793, he patented a mechanical device for winding yarns into thick ropes, based on a method he had seen natives using to make ropes in the West Indies. Three more patents followed, the last in 1805, as Huddart improved his machine. Ropes capable of taking great tensions were in demand and his new

Brynkir Tower,
built to impress a king
and today a luxury
holiday cottage

steam-driven machine was an instant success. Huddart was becoming fabulously wealthy. A commentator wrote, shortly after his death, 'Of his skills in mechanism, he has left a monument in the machinery for the manufacture of cordage, unrivalled in this or any other country.'

In 1809, Huddart purchased the 12,000 acre Bryncir Estate near Cricieth, and extended the sixteenth-century hall. The seagoing inventor died seven years later, leaving his fortune and the estate to his son, also named Joseph. George IV was crowned in 1820 and when the new owner of Bryncir heard that his monarch was visiting north Wales he decided to build a grandiose tower on the estate to celebrate the occasion. The six-storey tower folly was built in a Gothic style and designed to impress. The tower must have pleased the king because he knighted Joseph Huddart during the visit.

Sir Joseph and his wife produced nine children. When he died in 1841 his eldest son, George Augustus, became the owner of Bryncir. Like his father, George was a family man and had ten children. But any tranquillity at Bryncir was about to be shattered. Sir Clough Williams-Ellis, famous for creating Portmeirion, recorded in his autobiography:

> My Uncle Dick told me how as a boy, alerted by rumour, he had gone up to Bryncir, which he found completely deserted by both family and staff. Prowling round and pressing his nose against the dining-room windows he saw a large table all laid for breakfast, obviously hurriedly abandoned with eggs half eaten, tea cups half full and chairs all anyhow.

Like the crew of the *Marie Celeste*, the people had vanished.

At first it was believed one of George's sons had run off with the family governess and everyone had left the house in hot pursuit. More recently, it has been suggested that George Huddart was maintaining a secret family, and when its existence was discovered a furious row resulted in the house emptying. The couple never divorced but George moved to London and his wife retreated to Sussex. The children tried a number of times to return to Bryncir but, because of the continuing unpleasantness, never did. Some, it has been claimed, moved to Australia where they established the Huddart Parker Shipping Company.

Bryncir Hall was sold in 1903 and the estate broken up. During World War I, the hall was used as a prisoner-of-war camp; the eventually empty building, was demolished shortly after the Second World War. By the 1990s, the Gothic tower was a rotten shell of a building but extensive repairs and a creative restoration converted the folly into a luxury high-rise holiday cottage, ideal for those who want to pamper themselves in Gothic splendour in a tower built to impress a king.

22

Fort Williamsburg
Glynllifon

When in 1549, John Wynn was King Edward VI's standard bearer the king rewarded him with a gift of Bardsey Island. In the seventeenth century, his descendant, Thomas Wynn, married Francis Glynne, sole heiress to Glynllifon, uniting their two powerful estates. Yet more land was acquired, making the Glynllifon Wynns the most prominent family in Caernarfonshire.

Two hundred years passed until, their descendant Thomas Wynn, born in 1736, inherited the substantial fortune. He married Maria Stella Patronialla, who claimed that her father was Louis Philippe, Duke of Orleans – later the King of France. Her claim was never proved. By the age of twenty-five, Thomas had been knighted, become a Member of Parliament, was the Constable of Caernarfon Castle and Lord Lieutenant of the County; duties he took seriously.

The Militia Act of 1757 allowed auxiliary forces to be raised to defend the realm, independently of the regular army. Sir Thomas, an eccentric, was of the opinion that the Lord Lieutenant of the County needed a fort and so he built one in the grounds of his estate. He named the new bastion Fort Williamsburg and, on 22 September 1761 – the day of King George III's coronation – Sir Thomas published laws and an

The watchtower at Fort Williamsburg looks out from the abandoned fort

enrolment book for the garrison. The rules for the garrison were based on the principles of 'Freedom, Firmness and Friendship'. There was also a female branch of the garrison known as 'The Holy Order of Sisterhood'.

The rectangular fort built by Sir Thomas contained a parade ground, magazine and tunnels linking the surrounding earthworks and a watchtower. Batteries of cannon lined the ramparts. It resembled a real military establishment, complete with soldiers, but had no practical defensive purpose.

The American War of Independence had started, in 1775, and France was supporting the colonial rebels. War in Europe was becoming a distinct possibility. The king signed a warrant allowing Sir Thomas to mobilise his militia. In 1776, Sir Thomas was elevated to the peerage as Lord Newborough. The French revolution started in 1792, and the following year King Louis XVI and his family were executed. Britain's aristocracy watched with horror as thousands of French nobles went to the guillotine and

Paris streets ran with blood. Would the French 'reign of terror' travel across the channel? In 1797 the French Republic sent a fleet to Wales and landed an army at Fishguard. The invasion failed but the warning was clear: the Republic of France was an enemy.

Lord Newborough examined Gwynedd's defences and decided that an improved coastal fort was needed at Llandwrog. The existing battery, Fort David, was inadequate, and Newborough built a new one at his own expense. The new fortification was named Fort Benlan and manned with militia from Fort Williamsburg. Williamsburg had been built for fun but Fort Benlan had a more serious purpose, to defend against a French attack. By now his Lordship's private force was called the Loyal Newborough Volunteers, and considered one of the best equipped regiments in the country.

The volunteers, although well equipped, were not, however, always properly rewarded. Records at the Royal Welch Fusiliers Museum include two bills presented to Lord Newborough in 1803 that went unpaid. It was the same year that the *London Gazette* reported Lord Newborough's promotion to the rank of Lieutenant Colonel. One bill was from Drill Sergeant William Jones for the men's training over a 137-week period at 10s 6d a week. The other, from Richard Thomas, was for cleaning weapons during the previous four years. He died before he was paid for polishing the muskets and his widow waited seven years for the debt to be settled. The receipt for £16 3s 9d that she signed in 1810 still exists.

Napoleon Bonaparte seized power in France in 1799 and proclaimed himself Emperor in 1804. Lord Newborough died three years later and was succeeded by his son. Europe was at war as Napoleon turned on neighbouring countries. He was finally stopped by a British and Prussian alliance at Waterloo in 1815. Despite Napoleon's defeat and exile to St Helena, France could not be trusted. As a precaution, Fort Benlan was reinforced with more cannon in 1824, but the expected invasion never came. Today, with the threat of attack long since gone, Fort Benlan is a group holiday home that can accommodate up to forty-five guests.

With no strategic importance, Fort Williamsburg was abandoned after Lord Newborough's death. It now stands empty, in the grounds of Glynllifon Agricultural College. The parade ground, armoury, ramparts, lookout tower and tunnels have all been listed as architecturally important, but the buildings continue to decay, a sad end to the little fort built by an eccentric gentleman.

23

Penrhyn Castle
Bangor

The biggest and possibly most controversial folly in Wales is Penrhyn Castle. Its Norman-style keep and battlements dominate the Menai Strait. Today the castle is enjoyed by thousands of visitors every year, who come to see attractions which include an industrial railway museum, a one-ton slate bed built for Queen Victoria to use during a stay, and galleries of paintings by Old Masters such as Rembrandt, Canaletto and Vecchio. The art collection is priceless. The Dutch Culture Ministry once tried to buy one of the Rembrandts but couldn't raise the £40m asking price. As well as visiting the house, day trippers explore the formal gardens and enjoy picnics while children run and jump in the adventure playground. The castle's sombre façade looks military enough but it isn't Norman at all. Penrhyn is a fantasy castle, built in the 1820s with money earned from the sweat of slaves in Jamaica and Welsh quarrymen who were treated little better than slaves by their master.

Richard Pennant 1st Baron Penrhyn was a Member of Parliament and ardent opponent of the abolition of slavery. The Baron had good reason to take the floor of the house and criticise the abolitionist; he owned six sugar plantations in Jamaica and counted more than 600 slaves amongst his chattels. Their ill-fortune

Penrhyn Castle

was making him wealthy. Baron Penrhyn preferred to live in Wales and control his sugar plantations by letter. In one letter, to a plantation manager, he wrote, 'I do not wish the cattle or the negroes to be overworked.' Included in the lists of slaves were three midwives kept to ensure a supply of healthy new slaves, essential to keep the plantations running and cheaper than buying replacements.

Baron Penrhyn had another source of income. He had married an heiress and acquired, as a result, more Welsh estates. His Welsh possessions included Penrhyn Slate Quarry. Welsh slate was highly prized and exported across the world and the quarry was a useful asset.

Richard Pennant died on 21 January 1808 and his entire estate was inherited by his second cousin

George Hay Dawkins, who promptly appended the name Pennant to his surname. Dawkins-Pennant was now immensely wealthy and, in 1822, commissioned the architect Thomas Hopper to build a mock Norman Castle at Penrhyn. Money was no object. Dawkins-Pennant had seen Gwrych Castle, the folly built by Lord Hesketh, three years earlier, and wanted something bigger and better.

Penrhyn Castle

Penrhyn Castle had to be taller and more imposing than Gwrych, its rooms more magnificent and its furniture more opulent. The transportation of slaves across the Atlantic had been made illegal in 1807 but slavery continued in Jamaica and there was plenty of money to pay for the extravagant castle Dawkins-Pennant wanted. One estimate put the cost of Penrhyn Castle at £150,000, which would be £49 million in today values.

In 1833 the abolitionists forced an act through Parliament abolishing slavery throughout the British Empire. Dawkins-Pennant's Jamaican cash-cow would never be as profitable again and he turned to Penrhyn Quarry. It would have to make up the lost revenue. Dawkins-Pennant died in 1840 and the estate passed through his daughter Juliana, who died two years later, to his son-in-law Colonel Edward Gordon Douglas. The terms of his inheritance required him to adopt the name of Pennant, which he duly did. Queen Victoria stayed at Penrhyn Castle in 1859, and shortly after her visit he was elevated to the peerage as Baron Penrhyn. The Baron continued to buy land and by 1871 he was one of the largest landowners in Wales. He died in 1886 and his son, the 2nd Baron, inherited. By 1899 his annual income from the quarry was £133,000 and Penryhn Quarry was the biggest slate quarry in the world. Its main excavation was over a mile long (1.6 km) and 1,200 ft deep (370 m), a hole which was being dug by 3,000 men.

The Baron treated his men with contempt. They had gone on strike in 1896 demanding better pay and conditions, but he refused to concede to any demands. The strike lasted for eleven months before collapsing. After the strike Baron Penrhyn sacked the ringleaders and intimidated the remaining men, threatening them with the loss of their jobs. His heavy handed attitude triggered a second strike, which began on 22 November 1900. The men's demands were for a minimum wage, the right to save for a sick club, union representation, the reinstatement of victimised men and improved safety in the quarry. Baron Penrhyn was in an uncompromising mood and ignored the demands.

World demand for slate had reduced and the baron decided to wait the men out. After six months some drifted back, but the strike continued. There were bitter arguments between the strikers, whose families were starving, and the men who had gone back to work. The reduced workforce and lower demand for slate suited the baron. The men held out for three years before they were forced to give up the fight. They went back without winning a single concession. It had been the longest industrial dispute in history and left deep scars in the community, which are still evident a hundred years later.

In 2007 an exhibition was planned at Penrhyn Castle to celebrate the centenary of the ending of the slave trade but local feeling was still hostile towards the Pennant family because of his treatment of the quarrymen. To avoid any upset it was decided to include a display about the strike and its consequences on the workers.

In 1907 the 2nd Baron Penrhyn passed away and his son sold off parts of the estate. The Jamaican sugar plantations were sold in 1933; in 1951 Penrhyn Castle was passed to the Treasury in lieu of death duties. The castle was then transferred to the National Trust to be preserved and enjoyed by the public. In 1973 Lady Janet Douglas-Pennant sold her last remaining shares in Penrhyn Quarry, ending a family association which had lasted over 250 years.

24

Maenan Hall Gazebo
Llanrwst

Morus ap Dafydd, born about 1530, was, apparently, the illegitimate son of an educated priest named Sir David Owen. His father rented a house from Maenan Abbey and, like other clerics, made a very good living from his religious activities. In 1534, King Henry VIII proclaimed himself Supreme Head of the Church, dissolved the monasteries, and seized their assets. Nine years after the dissolution, Morus' father bought the monastery land and when Edward VI offered Anglican clergymen a licence to marry, overturning the rules of celibacy, his parents wed. The family, now firmly Church of England, continued to live at Maenan.

Morus received a good education and was a precocious youth, quick to learn different languages. While still a teenager he translated the Roman comedy *Andria* (*The Girl from Andros*) from its Latin text into English. Morus also wrote English and Welsh poetry. When his father died in 1558 Morus inherited Maenan. He then changed his name to Maurice Kyffin and invented a new past. The *Dictionary of Eminent Welshmen*, published by Canon Robert Williams, declares that Maurice was the second son of Richard Kyffin Esquire, but his assertion is generally disputed. Morus Owen had become Maurice Kyffin, gentleman.

Maenan Hall Gazebo complete with statue

In the sixteenth century, having the wrong religious views was dangerous, and Maurice Kyffin was 'adaptable' in his spiritual observances. During the reigns of Henry VIII and his son Edward VI, Kyffin was a Protestant, a Catholic during Queen Mary's reign, and a Protestant once more when Elizabeth I succeeded her half-sister. As well as keeping on the right side of the religious divide, Maurice was ambitious and sent poetry to Queen Elizabeth. He married twice, the second time to Margaret Mostyn from Flintshire who bore him eight children. It was the beginning of a Kyffin dynasty that would expand across north Wales. In 1580, Maurice became the High Sheriff of Caernarfon and built Maenan Hall, a new house suitable for the man of rank he had become. The gazebo that stands 100 metres south-east of Maenan Hall is shown on a 1900 Ordnance Survey map and was built some time during the eighteenth century. It's a circular brick tower containing a statue and there is a spiral staircase around the outside, probably a later addition. There is no record of who had constructed the folly but the last Kyffin to live at Maenan Hall was Sir Thomas Kyffin, who died in 1784. Following his death, the house went into decline.

In 1946, Maenan Hall was bought by the 2nd Lord Aberconway, the owner of Bodnant, to be used as a dower house for his wife Christabel. After buying the hall, the couple began the mammoth task of restoring it and clearing the overgrown gardens. Lord Aberconway died in 1953, but his wife continued to improve the gardens, and remained a resident at Maenan Hall until her death in 1974. Today, Maenan Hall and the gazebo are listed buildings owned by the McLaren family, descendants of Lord and Lady Aberconway. The McLarens have continued to maintain the gardens and open them to the public on certain days of the year.

25

'The Poem' and the Pin Mill
Bodnant, Colwyn Bay

Henry Davis Pochin, a farmer's son, trained as an apprentice chemist in Manchester and went into business with his employer. When his partner died, Pochin became sole proprietor and went on to invent a process to clarify a brown resin called rosin. The clarified resin made it possible to manufacture white soap. Pochin sold the rights to his invention and used the proceeds to develop another idea: using alumina to manufacture paper. The second invention required china clay and Pochin purchased china clay quarries to supply the raw material.

Eventually, his business H. D. Pochin and Co. was absorbed into the English China Clay Group. In 2000 the company was bought by Imetal SA, now called Imerys, who have since become the largest china clay producers in the world. Henry Pochin was also a director of the Tredegar Iron and Coal Company and the Staveley Coal and Iron Company. One of the Tredegar mines was named 'Laura', after his daughter who married Charles McLaren, later to become the 1st Baron Aberconway.

Henry Pochin was a keen gardener. In 1874, he purchased the Bodnant Estate and, having partially retired, began to develop the stunning gardens that exist today. Towards the southern end of the garden,

The Pin Mill's beauty is reflected in the canal

in a secluded spot overlooking a millpond, he constructed an unusual Gothic tower and had the words 'The Poem' carved on the masonry above the entrance doors. Henry Pochin died in 1895, aged seventy-one, and his body was interred in a crypt beneath the tower. 'The Poem,' as he had named it, was a mausoleum for himself and his family. No records exist to explain the name but it is believed to stand for 'Place of Eternal Memory.' Following his death, Bodnant passed to his daughter and her husband Charles. They continued to improve the gardens. Charles McLaren, who was now the Chairman of the Tredegar Company, was ennobled by King George VI on 21 June 1911.

The Pin Mill has a strange history. It's believed to have been built around 1720 as a summer house in a Woodchester country estate, before falling into disuse. It was then employed as a factory where dress making pins were manufactured and finally the repository for hides waiting to be soaked in urine to cure.

Henry, the 2nd Baron Aberconway, had always liked the building and wanted to save it. He started a fund to restore it but there was little interest. No one else wanted the Pin Mill, so in 1938 the baron had it carefully dismantled and transported to Bodnant, where it was rebuilt. He commissioned the prominent architect, J. Murray Easton, to alter the Pin Mill to improve its appearance. Carpenters from the

The Poem Mausoleum at Bodnant is still used as a family mausoleum

John Brown shipyard on Clydebank, where Henry was Chairman, built a new staircase for the folly.

The location chosen for the Pin Mill, at one end of the Canal Terrace, has created a visual delight as the reflection from the water mirrors the mill itself.

The McLaren family still live at Bodnant and the gardens are in the care of the National Trust and open to the public. 'The Poem' has recently undergone structural repairs, funded by Cadw, and continues to be used as a family mausoleum. Charles, the 3rd Lord Aberconway, was laid to rest in 'The Poem' in 2003. Although the mausoleum is still in use, the curious are allowed inside on certain days of the week.

On the Canal Terrace, visitors enjoy the Pin Mill in its latest setting, which isn't bad for a building that has been saved from destruction and recycled three times.

26

Fishguard Fort

Sitting on a promontory between the old harbour of Fishguard and the larger new commercial dock is a grassy mound, some stone ruins and a battery of ancient cannon. This is Fishguard Fort and it has an interesting story to tell. It begins on the 10th May 1773 when the British government passed a law taxing tea throughout the empire. The new tax enraged American colonialists who disguised themselves as Red Indians, boarded a ship in Boston harbour and dumped the cargo of tea into the sea shouting, 'No taxation without representation'. The tax was going to Britain where the colonists had no elected politicians to speak for them. The event, sometimes called 'The Boston Tea Party' triggered other demonstrations; talk of rebellion was in the air. There were more acts of revolt and hostilities quickly turned violent. In 1776 the Americans rejected the monarchy, calling the king a tyrant and declared themselves an independent nation. The American War of Independence had begun.

Without any warships of its own, the Americans began to issue 'Letters of Marque' to private ship owners giving them licence to attack British vessels seizing the ships and cargo for profit. These privateers, and there were more than 1,700 of them, were well armed and the crews hungry for plunder.

A row of canons at Fishguard Fort

One of the most audacious was a Yankee privateer called the 'Black Prince'. Britain had the biggest merchant fleet in the world and the Black Prince would lurk along the west coast of the British Isles to surprise unsuspecting vessels. In 1779 the privateer sailed into Fishguard with a captured cargo ship and a ransom demand. Her captain wanted the town to pay £1000 or he would open fire. When the people of Fishguard refused to pay the American bombarded the town, causing considerable damage.

Determined never again to be defenceless, the people built a fort above the harbour, installed eight nine pound cannons and hired three invalid gunners from Woolwich Arsenal to keep watch, manning the guns in case of another attack. None came and in 1783

*One of the canons
from the fort now placed
in the centre of Fishguard*

the war with America ended. With the arrival of peace the fort was no longer considered important and allowed to deteriorate, an error which nearly had serious consequences.

On Wednesday 22nd February 1797 a squadron of warships was spotted off the coast flying British flags but there was something odd about the ships and a hurried alarm was raised. Next, a French Frigate, the Resistance sailed into Fishguard Bay and was fired upon by a 9lb cannon in the fort whereupon she withdrew, unaware that the fort only had 3 round of shot in its magazine. Unwilling to attack the fort, the French Fleet anchored at Carregwastad Point and disembarked 1400 men and arms including 40 barrels of gunpowder and several thousand rifles. At least one boat capsized and all the invaders' 4-pound cannons were lost. Having unloaded, the French fleet withdrew. An invading French army was ashore and ready to advance, attacking as it went.

What happened next is well recorded and has

become part of Welsh folklore. The leader of the local volunteer militia, a young headstrong Colonel by the name of Knox, gathered together a few men, armed with an assortment of crude weapons and set off along the cliff path, followed by curious townsfolk. Seeing a long line of what they thought were British Red Coat soldiers advancing along the cliff, the French retreated inland. They were mistaken. There were no regular troops, only women dressed in traditional red capes and

'The French Invasion'
on a tavern sign
in Fishguard

tall black hats. No longer feeling quite so confident and realising his small band of ill equipped men was no match for the enemy, Colonel Knox also withdrew. Believing they faced the might of the British army the French surrendered the following day. After the surrender Jemima Nicholas, a 47-year-old cobbler from Fishguard known to all as Jemima Fawr (Big Jemima) took it upon herself to take a pitchfork, round up 12 French deserters and lock them in St. Mary's Church. With her help and the boldness of the Welsh people the last invasion of Britain ended.

Having fired one cannon ball in anger, Fishguard Fort never saw action again. It was manned until the end of the Napoleonic Wars, in 1815 and then allowed to fall into disrepair. Today, it is owned by Pembrokeshire Coast National Park and is a lovely place to stop, picnic and enjoy the stunning views across Fishguard bay.

27

Trevor Tower
Llangollen

Trevor Hall lies east of Llangollen, not far from the Pontcysyllte aqueduct. John Trevor, Bishop of Asaph, who, in 1345, built the bridge in Llangollen crossing the Dee, was an important man, and the hall and Trevor Tower are named after him. In 1715, his descendant, Mary Trevor, married, and the estate passed to John Lloyd from Montgomeryshire. The Lloyds rebuilt the hall and expanded it.

The Lloyd male line ended early in the nineteenth century and the hall passed, again by marriage, to Rice Thomas who, in 1820, rented out the hall. A series of tenants occupied Trevor Hall, including a shipping broker from Liverpool, the manager of a local ironworks, and James Edwards, High Sheriff of Denbighshire.

The folly, Trevor Tower, situated in a wood north of the hall, was built in 1827 by George Hammond Whalley, MP for Peterborough. (Whalley was a direct descendant of the regicide, Edward Whalley who, in 1649, had signed King Charles I's death warrant.) George Whalley was a well-educated, ambitious and intelligent man. As well as being a parliamentarian, he was a barrister, Chairman of the Llanidloes and Newtown Railway, Captain of the Denbighshire Yeomanry, an ardent Anglican, active in the

Trevor Tower built by the vitriolic anti catholic MP George Whalley now looks sad and neglected

Temperance League and, less creditably, anti-Catholic.

For some reason, Whalley named his folly tower King William's Tower, after the eleventh-century king, William Rufus. Today, Ordnance Survey maps refer to the tower as 'Trevor Tower', while the Royal Commission on the Ancient and Historical Monuments of Wales still call the folly 'King William's Tower'. The circular, three-storey tower has a castellated roof and a small turret at the top. What use Whalley intended for the tower is not known, but it may have been as a hunting lodge or a summer house.

George Whalley's politics were extreme. There were a number of fraudulent irregularities during his elections and he was twice voided as an MP following complaints and enquiries. One of Whalley's parliamentary campaigns was against the Maynooth Grant, a British government fund supporting a Catholic seminary in Maynooth, Ireland. Whalley claimed that Britain was 'paying for the creation of priests whose goal was to turn Britain into a citadel of popery'. His vitriolic attacks were shouted down by Irish MPs. Later, in 1866, Whalley became even more extreme and bizarrely claimed that the Vatican had militarily interfered in New Zealand to defeat British forces, planned to usurp the crown with a Catholic pretender, and were in control of parts of the army, the police, the telegraph system and the railways. His outbursts drew public attention and he was lampooned as 'The Great Believer in Roman Catholicism' in the newspapers.

Whalley also supported and campaigned on behalf of Arthur Orton, known as the Tichborne Claimant. When Roger Tichborne, an heir to a large fortune and a baronetcy, vanished during a shipwreck his mother advertised, trying to locate her son, believing him to have made his way to Australia. A butcher from Wagga Wagga, Australia, came forward claiming to be the lost Tichborne and the grieving woman embraced him as her lost son. The rest of the Tichborne family smelt a rat and a notorious legal case ended when a jury decided that the claimant, supported by Whalley, was an impostor named Orton. Arthur Orton was a London butcher who had emigrated to Australia. Orton (or, according to his supporters, the doubly-unfortunate missing son) was convicted of perjury and sent to prison for fourteen years for lying under oath about his impersonation of Roger Tichborne.

George Whalley died in 1878 while still a Member of Parliament. He was insolvent. Trevor Hall has recently been carefully restored and is now promoted as a luxury stately home for hire. Whalley's legacy, the Trevor Tower, stands alone in a dark wood, looking dishevelled and a bit ridiculous, much as the man himself must have looked towards the end of his political career.

28

The Gothic Water Tower
Lake Vyrnwy

There is an impressive Gothic tower surrounded by water near the B4393 in what is now Powys. Driving past, you might be forgiven for thinking it is a fairytale castle where a princess with long flowing hair was once held prisoner until her true love came to rescue her. The tower, with its battlements and pointed copper-clad roofs, is a work of art, built in a time when appearance was as important as function and cost was a secondary consideration. The truth is that the fairytale castle, which would not look out of place in Eastern Europe, is nothing more than a water filtering plant. The story of why such a beautiful building was built is a potent reminder of Welsh Nationalism.

In the 1950s, the Welsh politician Gwynfor Evans campaigned to stop the damming of the Tryweryn. He failed and the inhabitants of the village of Capel Celyn were forcibly removed from their homes, which were then flooded so that a reservoir supplying Liverpool and the Wirral could be built. It was not the first or last time that a Welsh community would be evicted from its land to feed the voracious thirst for water of a big city across the border.

Liverpool had grown rich from the slave trade, but although trading in slaves had been made illegal in 1807 it still went on. Slavery in British colonies

The 160ft (39m)Gothic Tower from where 54 million gallons of water a day leave for Liverpool

continued until it was abolished in 1833. However, the demise of the slave trade did not stop Liverpool growing. Irish immigrants, escaping the potato famine, flooded into Liverpool, and the city's docks expanded exponentially to handle the trade in cotton, to and from the textile mills of Manchester and Lancashire. There was an influx of Welshmen, too, who built factories and houses. It is estimated that during the eighteenth century the population of the city grew from 6,000 people to 80,000. By 1901, 700,000 souls would live in Liverpool.

New water supplies were desperately needed, to cater for the rapidly expanding city and the authorities looked west, to Wales, for a solution. Abundant rainfall and mountainous terrain that made building dams practical made Wales the ideal answer. A site was chosen in Montgomeryshire (now in the county of Powys) and dam construction began in 1881. Locals in the little village of Llanddwyn watched in wonder as a huge stone wall was built across their valley. It took 1,000 men, using steam-powered machinery, seven years to complete the dam and, in 1888, the valley began to fill with water. It was the first high stone dam to be built in the United Kingdom and cost more than £600,000 – more than £22m in today's values. There was another, human, price to pay for such an ambitious project. A small obelisk stands near the dam, to commemorate the forty-four men killed during its construction.

More dams using a similar design would be built in Wales in years to come.

As the water level behind the dam began to rise, a new village was built lower down the valley. Four hundred occupants, whose properties were about to be flooded, were moved to new homes. Even the dead, who had been laid to rest in the village graveyard, were dug up and moved. In all thirty-seven farmhouses, three taverns, two chapels, two shops, a post office and assorted dwellings were demolished. It took two years to fill the reservoir. Slowly, the village of Llanddwyn vanished beneath the surface and, in its place, a new majestic building rose up 160 feet (49 metres), from the side of the valley. This was the water tower, whose purpose was to filter the water and send it on its way to Liverpool.

Once the valves were opened, fifty-four million

gallons of drinking water left the tower each day, travelling along a 2¼-mile tunnel whence it continued a further 75 miles along pipes and aqueducts to its final destination. The entire journey, including the section of pipes carrying the water beneath the Mersey, was driven by gravity.

Today, the magnificent stone dam and its Gothic water tower stand as evidence of the confidence and ambition of Victorian engineers who would let nothing stand in their way. Since its construction, the stonework has mellowed, nature has reclaimed the surrounding landscape, and Lake Vyrnwy (*Llyn Efyrnwy*) has become a place of exceptional beauty. Below the dam, a sculpture park has been created. There are lakeside walks and picnic sites. A nature reserve, managed by the RSPB, now exists beside the reservoir and the area is a popular destination for hikers, sailors, cyclists, rock climbers and fishermen. Lake Vyrnwy has been stocked with 400,000 Loch Leven trout. The new village of Llanwddyn has flourished, benefitting from the influx of visitors attracted by the dam; 125 years after it was built, the fairytale water tower continues to send drinking water to the thirsty people of Liverpool. However, not all of it is drunk straight away. Some of the water, you may be pleased to learn, is used to distil a refreshing tipple known as Bombay Sapphire Gin.

29

Rodney's Pillar
Welshpool

George Brydges Rodney joined the navy in 1732 at the age of fourteen. A mix of ability and the patronage of James Brydges, Duke of Chandos, led to rapid promotion, and by 1745 George was in command of *HMS Ludlow Castle*, having been promoted as the youngest captain in the Royal Navy. The *Ludlow Castle*, which had just been commissioned, patrolled the Scottish coast during the Jacobite rebellion. One of his midshipmen in the crew was Samuel Hood who went on to have an illustrious career and after whom *HMS Hood*, sunk by the German battleship *Bismark*, was named.

Rodney's next vessel was the 60-gun *HMS Eagle* which he commanded during an engagement to capture a Spanish privateer. Prize money from the sale of captured enemy ships was a lucrative business and Rodney saw the possibility of making himself rich. Later, while returning from Ireland, he ignored an order and instead chased a convoy of French merchantmen capturing six ships. The war with France continued until 1748 when a treaty signalled the end of hostilities. By then, his prize money from captured shipping amounted to £15,000, making him financially secure for life (£25m in today's values).

The outbreak of peace left Rodney out of work until

The golden globe at the top of Rodney's Pillar has gone, destroyed during a lightening strike

he secured the post of commander-in-chief of Newfoundland and became the MP for Saltash, an admiralty-controlled safe seat. With England and France competing for America, peace was unlikely to last, and fighting started again in 1754. Rodney was soon back at sea and in action. In 1759, after a series of naval battles he was promoted to Rear Admiral. The war with France dragged on until 1763.

In 1764, Admiral Rodney was elevated to a baronetcy and returned home to pursue his political ambitions. As well as being a Member of Parliament, at the time an unpaid position (parliamentary salaries were not introduced until 1911), Rodney was appointed Rear Admiral of Great Britain and Admiral of the White, but the post was again without salary. Heavy spending on election campaigns, extravagant gambling and expensive tastes quickly consumed his fortune and, hounded by creditors, Rodney retreated to live in Paris. Eventually, with the help of influential friends, he obtained a salaried command and returned to pay his debts.

The American War of Independence resulted in Admiral Rodney returning to active duty and he took part in a series of actions culminating in the Battle of Saintes when, in 1782, he smashed the French fleet using the tactic of breaking the enemy line by sailing through it, instead of alongside, to engage. It was the same tactic that Admiral Nelson would employ so successfully at Trafalgar twenty-three years later.

Admiral Rodney struck his flag and retired shortly after the Battle of Saintes, when parliament voted him a pension of £2,000 per annum. He died ten years later in 1792. When he retired, Rodney was a national hero. Parents christened their sons Rodney. Newfoundland round-bottomed boats became known as Rodneys. In his honour, seven Royal Navy ships have been called *HMS Rodney*. There is a Rodney Bay in St Lucia, an Admiral Rodney Extra Old Rum, a Rodney Street in Liverpool, numerous Admiral Rodney public houses, and Rodney's Pillar in Montgomeryshire.

The reason the notable people of Montgomeryshire decided to erect a stone pillar high on Breidden Hill, miles from any sea, is because of trees. The ancient oak forests that grew in the Welsh borders were an important source of raw materials needed for the construction of fighting ships of the line. Once the trees from Montgomeryshire were felled they were dragged to the Severn and floated downstream to the shipyards of Bristol, where shipwrights crafted the 'Men o' War' that ruled the waves. The sale of so much timber to the naval dockyards made local landowners particularly appreciative of Rodney's exploits.

Rodney's Pillar was officially opened in 1782 by Mrs Eyton, Lady of the Manor, accompanied by musicians and a large crowd of dignitaries. According to one account, there was originally a Welsh inscription on the pillar, which (when translated) read:

The highest pillars will fall. The strongest towers will decay but the fame of Sir George Brydges Rodney shall increase continually and his good name shall never be obliterated.

Rodney's supporters mounted a golden ball on the top of the pillar and held annual picnics during the 1800s to toast the admiral and sing of his exploits.

In 1835, a lightning strike destroyed the golden ball. A copper substitute was fitted in 1847, but this has not survived. The Welsh inscription has also vanished, replaced by the words:

Erected in honour of Sir George Bryden Rodney, Admiral of the White, by subscription of the gentlemen of Montgomery 1781. Repaired 1847. Renewed 1896 by subscription of gentlemen of the counties of Montgomery and Salop.

Why Admiral Rodney's middle name was inscribed as 'Bryden' on the folly when his name was Brydges is unclear.

The pillar has been repaired several times since 1896, lastly in 1984.

Admiral Rodney was vain, self-important and unscrupulous in his pursuit of prize money. His protégé Hood, who had risen to the rank of Admiral, accused Rodney of 'Sacrificing the interests of the service to his own profit'. Others accused him of nepotism after he promoted his 15-year-old son to the rank of Post Captain, a rank that could command a frigate or similar-sized ship. Despite these faults Rodney was an able naval officer, a hero of his age, and a notable character who helped create British maritime supremacy.

30

Leighton Hall Gateway
Welshpool

In 1845, Christopher Leyland, a Liverpool banker, purchased Leighton Hall, near Welshpool (*Trallwng*), and gave it to his nephew John Naylor as a wedding present. Naylor, himself a banker and one of the richest men in Britain, rebuilt the Hall and employed Augustus Pugin, the interior designer of the Houses of Parliament, to add the finishing touches. A set of three magnificent Gothic arches, set back from the road, created a suitably imposing gateway leading to the deer park and hall. Naylor believed in using modern technology, and wanted to bring the 4,000 acres of farmland on his new estate up to date by using the very latest agricultural ideas.

Naylor built Nantcribba, a model farm, where he could use test new inventions and ideas. Nantcribba had its own water-turbine generating electricity, a gasworks that lit Leighton Hall, a mill producing flour and animal feeds, a wheelright, sawmills, a blacksmith's shop, cottages to house his labourers, and a funicular railway transporting farmyard slurry to storage tanks. It took him eight years to complete the project.

As well as being an advocate and practitioner of agricultural advance, Naylor was interested in horticulture and spent money redesigning the hall's

Leighton Hall Gateway, Gothic splendour built by
John Naylor, one of the richest men in Britain

gardens and park. He employed the designer Edward Kemp to remodel the gardens and searched for exotic trees to decorate the park. A record of Naylor's improvements to the gardens, written with gold leaf on vellum, is stored at the National Library of Wales. Kemp included two varieties of conifer in the scheme. In the wild the Monterey Cypress and the Nootka or Alaskan Cypress existed thousands of miles apart, but at Leighton Hall they were planted in close proximity. When the trees cross-pollinated in 1888 an entirely new species was created, which Naylor named *Cupressocyparis leylandii* after his generous uncle.

John Naylor died shortly afterwards and Leighton Hall passed to his son Christopher, a master mariner.

Christopher and his younger brother continued developing the new species. They reverse-pollinated and cloned the young Leylandii to create more hybrids. When John Naylor's widow died in 1909, death duties forced the sale of some of the estate. In 1931, John Naylor's grandson sold Leighton Hall and moved away.

The hall remained a private home until after the Second World War, when it served as a boys' school, during which time much of the garden architecture was destroyed or removed, and the ornamental lake was converted into a swimming pool. Then, for a short period, Leighton Hall was an arts foundation before returning to private ownership. In the 1990s the hall was sold again and, having been restored, remains a private residence.

John Naylor's legacy to farming is apparent, but his other gift to the nation, the Leylandii cypress tree, is more problematic. In the 1920s, nurserymen were looking for fast-growing trees, and the Forestry Commission began to plant Naylor's hybrids. Capable of growing more than 3 feet (1 metre) a year, Leylandii soon became popular with gardeners demanding instant privacy without ugly fences. Before long, Leylandii were the biggest-selling plants in garden centres across the UK.

What gardeners with modest plots did not appreciate was the trees' potential to grow up to 66 feet (35 metres) tall. Within years huge trees were blocking sunlight from people's homes, smothering other plants, ruining gardens and creating misery. By

2005, an estimated 17,000 neighbours were quarrelling over hedges that were out of control. In 2001, a pensioner in Talybont-on-Usk (*Tal-y-bont ar Wysg*) was shot dead during a heated argument about a Leylandii boundary hedge; in 2008 Christine Wright won a 24-year courtroom battle to have her neighbour's trees removed. Today, the Anti Social Behaviour Act of 2003 gives local authorities powers to shorten or remove problem hedges.

Leighton Hall gates may now be closed to the public, but they remain as a folly and a reminder of John Naylor, a man of vision who unintentionally created a gardening nightmare for thousands.

31

The Wellington Monument
Aberystwyth

Look south from the harbour at Aberystwyth and you will see, on a hill in the distance, a pillar which looks like an enormous cannon that has been stood on its end. The monument was erected on Pen Dinas, in the 1850s, as a memorial to the Duke of Wellington. Pen Dinas (*pen*: top; *dinas*: hillfort) had once been the highest part of an Iron Age hill fort and, according to legend, the home of the giant Maelor Gawr. To understand why the residents of a Welsh Victorian seaside town like Aberystwyth would go to the expense of erecting a monument to an Anglo-Irish soldier we need to look back 200 years.

Arthur Wellesley was born in Dublin in 1769, the fourth son of the 1st Earl of Mornington. He was educated in Ireland and then at Eton. While he was still at school, his father died leaving the family short of money. The young Arthur was taken to Brussels to continue his education on a more limited budget. He returned to England in 1786, having become a proficient horseman and able to speak French. Without money there were few ways for a young man to make his way in society and Arthur's mother approached the Duke of Rutland, a family friend, for help in finding a position for her son. He arranged for

*Wellington Monument, built in the shape of an
upturned cannon to celebrate the Battle of Waterloo*

Arthur to be commissioned as an ensign in the army.
Young army officers had few duties: Arthur's military
career started in Dublin, where he spent his time
socialising, gambling and getting into debt.

Promotion followed. During the next twenty years
Arthur Wellesley proved himself a talented battlefield
tactician and leader of men. He saw action in the
Netherlands, India and Denmark. By 1808 he was a
general with a series of military victories to prove how
capable he was. In addition to his military career
Arthur Wellesley pursued political ambitions. He
served as a Member of Parliament, Secretary of State
for Ireland and became a Privy Councillor.

In 1808 Wellesley commanded an army that
engaged the French in a series of battles known as the

Peninsular Wars. The wars ended in 1813 with the French Emperor Napoleon Bonaparte being defeated, abdicating, and being exiled to the island of Elba. General Wellesley was hailed as the victor and a grateful country created him Duke of Wellington. He had spent six years fighting a long and bloody campaign against the French.

A short period of peace followed, but in 1815 Napoleon escaped from Elba, returned to France, regained control and raised a new army. It was clear that he had to be stopped, and British forces quickly mobilised in alliance with a Prussian army. On 18 June 1815 the allied armies confronted Napoleon's Imperial French army at a small town named Waterloo. Wellington had 67,000 troops under his command but many of them were inexperienced conscripts.

Napoleon's army comprised 69,000 men, most of whom were battle hardened veterans from the Peninsular Wars eager for a fight. They wanted to avenge their earlier defeats and give the British a bloody nose.

The battle began early in the morning and continued with ferocious fighting throughout the day. As dusk fell, 47,000 men lay dead on the battlefield and the French army had been destroyed. Throughout the night, small groups of exhausted, frightened soldiers huddled together on the battlefield, surrounded by dead bodies and listening to the cries of wounded men calling for water somewhere in the dark. There was no water and no comfort for the dying. Others scavenged the dead and wounded for valuables. Later, teeth were removed from the corpses, packed into barrels and sent back to Britain to be made into dentures.

It was a resounding victory for Wellington and the end of Napoleon's reign. The defeated Emperor was exiled again, this time to St Helena, a small island far out in the Atlantic from which there was no escape. He died there, in 1821, either of a stomach ulcer or, as some historians claim, by arsenic poisoning.

The victory at Waterloo cemented Wellington's reputation as a national hero. Following the battle, he resumed his political career and went on to serve as Prime Minister. The Duke of Wellington retired from public life in 1846 and died aged eighty-three in 1852. During Wellington's military career he had taken part in more than sixty battles. He was given the honour of a state funeral and buried in St Paul's Cathedral next to Lord Nelson.

Memorials and statues to the Duke of Wellington were commissioned across the land. In Aberystwyth a Mr W. E. Richards campaigned for one to be erected in memory of the great man.

The monument, which took the form of a 60 feet (18 metres) tall cannon, pointing skyward, was completed in about 1858. Some accounts suggest that a statue of Wellington, mounted on his horse, was intended to be placed on the top of the monument. But funds ran out, and the statue of Wellington, astride his charger, stayed in a stonemason's yard in Cardiff until it was eventually sold and used elsewhere.

Not everyone was impressed with the monument

on Pen Dinas. The 1874 edition of *New Guide to Aberystwyth* stated, 'Here a paltry monument, like a chimney stack, has been erected to the memory of the late Duke of Wellington'.

In 1976, repairs were carried out to the monument and a new lightning conductor was fitted, which was stolen shortly afterwards by scrap metal thieves. In 1997 a spectacular lightning strike hit the top of the tower, shattering some of the capping stones. The tower was restored in 1999, when a new topstone was fitted made of Blaenau Ffestiniog slate.

Today, the monument to the Duke of Wellington sits within Pen Dinas Nature Reserve and those who climb up to visit it are rewarded with stunning land- and seascapes.

32

The Richard Green-Price Obelisk
Knighton

Walkers following the Offa's Dyke path south of Knighton (*Trefyclawdd*) in Powys pass a granite obelisk in the middle of nowhere. The monument was erected in about 1890 in honour of Richard Green, a local lawyer and, according to some, a rather 'good egg'. Richard Green was born into a comfortable middle-class family on 18 October 1803. After an uneventful childhood, he trained as a solicitor and established a law practice at Knighton. The young solicitor was well connected: his uncle, Richard Price, was the local Member of Parliament, who had added to an already substantial fortune, during the sale and enclosure of Crown land in Radnorshire. Price was also the Lieutenant Colonel of the Radnorshire Militia, Lord of the Manor of Bleddfa and owner of Norton Manor. Richard Green was ambitious and eager to advance himself. A combination of hard work and patronage, not uncommon in those days, led to him being appointed Chairman of the local Health Board and Treasurer for the County of Radnorshire.

Once established, Green married and lived comfortably with his new wife in The Cottage, Knighton, but after just five years of marriage his wife, died leaving him a widower with two small children. Shortly afterwards he remarried and went on to have

The Richard Green-Price Obelisk remembers his services to the county of Radnor

thirteen more children with his second wife. In 1861, his uncle died and Richard Green inherited Norton Manor. In recognition of his uncle's benevolence, he added Price to his surname and the new Mr Green-Price moved with his expanding family into Norton Manor, their new home. Now wealthy, he turned his attention to politics and was elected to Parliament in 1863. As well as being an active parliamentarian Green-Price was an energetic constituency MP, heavily involved in an assortment of projects. At the same time, he improved his estate and built new houses for his tenants.

The nineteenth century was an age of rapid railway development. Fortunes were being made by shrewd investors, and Richard Green-Price was determined to take advantage of such a good opportunity. Local landowners banded together to bring a line from Craven Arms to Knighton, but not everyone was convinced it was a sound business idea. One letter read out at a public meeting said:

of the many unpromising schemes that are afloat, I think this is the most silly. There can be no passenger traffic and very little goods; and the capital, if any should be invested, will probably be sunk unprofitably.

The comments proved to be true and, it was said, the only people to prosper from the project were barristers, solicitors and brokers.

The railway struggled to attract passengers or freight and was taken over by the Central Wales Railway Company, who extended the line a further 20 miles to a station they called Llanerch Halt. From there, more track was added until the line reached Swansea. Seeing a new possibility for a profit, Green-Price bought land at Llanerch Halt and started to build property. It was a wise decision; he had bought at the right time. Llanerch Halt was about to become the new town of Llandrindod Wells. Visitors arriving on the new railway wanted to enjoy the health-giving waters of the town's spa, and Llandrindod Wells became a booming holiday resort.

Richard Green-Price used the money to extend his estate to more than 9,000 acres, yielding £7,000 of rent per annum. He was now an extremely wealthy man. In 1874 he was made 1st Baronet, Norton Manor and in 1876 became the High Sheriff of Radnorshire, a position which had existed since before the Norman invasion. It was abolished in 1974.

Richard Green-Price continued with his political career and fought his last election in 1886, aged eighty-two. He died the following year and was succeeded by his son, Richard Dansey Green-Price, who became the 2nd Baronet. Wanting to recognise the achievements of their long-standing Member of Parliament, the people of Knighton paid for a monument to be erected on Hengwn Hill, a lonely windswept hill 2 miles south of the town. Offa's Dyke passes nearby. The polished red granite obelisk is inscribed:

This public monument was erected by subscription to perpetuate the memory of Sir Richard Green Price 1st Baronet. Born 1803 died 1887. Whose services to the county of Radnor will long outlive his name.

The inscription, like the letter decrying the railway he proposed, contains an element of truth. Green-Price solicitors no longer practise in Knighton. Norton Manor, once Richard Green-Price's family home, is now a luxury hotel. In 1963, following a general review of the railway system, known as the 'Beeching Report,' the closure of the railway line at Knighton was proposed because it was unprofitable. Despite the threat, it survived, and the railway that Richard Green-Price was so keen to support is now a section of the Heart of Wales line, regarded by some as one of Britain's most picturesque routes.

Today, no freight travels along the line and the quiet of the Welsh countryside is disturbed each day by just four small passenger trains travelling from

Swansea to Shrewsbury and back. The route is so popular with pensioners, keen to enjoy a day out, that their concessionary free travel passes have been invalidated for this journey during summer months.

33

The Lewis Monument
New Radnor

Visitors to New Radnor (*Maesyfed*), Powys, are often surprised to discover a large monument in the village, which they sometimes mistake for a war memorial. The rather splendid 24 metres (77 feet) tall, Gothic style, structure would make a fitting memorial to the valiant dead of wars past but that is not its purpose. The Lewis Monument was built, by his admirers, to remind us of the achievements of one man.

Sir George Cornewall Lewis, 2nd Baronet, born 1806, came from local landed gentry. He was Educated at Eaton then Oxford and went on to become a lawyer, Member of Parliament, Chancellor of the Exchequer, Home Secretary and Secretary of State for War. Sir George was also a published writer and linguist responsible for translating a number of foreign works. As well as writing and translating, he was the editor of the *Edinburgh Review* and contributed essays to a variety of other publications. His political and judicial work included an enquiry into the condition of the Irish population, and a two-year visit to Malta to frame new codes of law for the island and its people. Sir George also served as one of the chief Poor-Law commissioners.

He was invited to Balmoral by Queen Victoria on several occasions, but always declined the offer.

Despite the snub, she made him a baronet in 1846. Sir George's incredible work rate continued and included published work on extradition laws, astronomy, Egyptology and the principles of government. He died in April 1863. Following Sir George's death, a number of monuments were erected to him including a marble bust in Westminster Abbey and a statue in Hereford, but all of these memorials are modest when compared with the enormous one put up in his home village of New Radnor. When it

The Lewis Monument, a grand monument to a man who didn't become Prime Minister

was unveiled, in 1864, the monument to the great man was the main front page feature of the newspaper *Illustrated London News*.

In the years since, interest in Sir George Cornewall Lewis has declined, and the monument at New Radnor has been neglected. No one, it seemed, wants to pay for its upkeep. By the 1990s, the Gothic structure was declared unsafe and fenced off to protect the general public from the risk of falling masonry. In January

1992, the Lewis Monument was made a Grade II listed building but it would be seven more years before the local authority finally agreed, in 1999, to pay for repair work to reinstate the memorial. As recently as July 2012, records of Community Council meetings show there were still discussions taking place with Cadw regarding further repairs that were needed.

In the view of the historian J. P. Parry, had he lived longer, Sir George would have become leader of the Liberal Party instead of William Gladstone, and the Gothic monument at New Radnor would be celebrating the life of Prime Minister Lewis, statesman and man of letters.

34

Tŵr y Deri – Derry Ormond Tower
New Radnor

In the eighteenth century, a country estate near Lampeter (*Llanbedr Pont Steffan*), known as Derry Ormond, was in financial difficulty. The owner David Jones, Sheriff of Cardiganshire, had died in 1775, owing a considerable amount of money. To clear his debts, Derry Ormond was put up for sale but there was little interest and it was not until 1783, eight years later, that a buyer was found. A London-based surgeon-apothecary named John Jones, no relation of the sheriff, acquired the estate for a paltry £1,575. He then expanded it, buying more land and building a new house for himself.

The new residents of Derry Ormond prospered, and John Jones' son, Thomas John Jones, formed a partnership to create the Banc y Llong (*llong*: ship), so called because of the ships featured on its bank notes. The official name of the business was the Aberystwyth and Cardiganshire Bank. The bank opened a branch office in London offering a service to Welsh drovers who, having driven large herds of livestock to England and sold the animals, needed to return the money they made to Wales. A £1 note from the Banc y Llong is kept in the National Museum of Wales at St Fagans. When Thomas died in 1817 his son, another John, inherited the estate together with a respectable fortune.

Tŵr y Deri – Derry Ormond Tower – constructed by a local squire to provide paid work for the unemployed men of the parish

While the Jones family had been making their fortune, Europe had been engaged in a long and bloody series of military campaigns known as the Napoleonic Wars. The wars ended in 1815 and the people across Europe looked forward to a period of peace and prosperity. Men put down their weapons. Swords were beaten into ploughshares and men across the continent returned to farming the land. Agricultural production leapt, causing a surplus of food. The price of corn and other staple foods collapsed and the world, including places as far from the conflict as America, went into recession.

As elsewhere, the farmers of Wales were faced with ruin. To survive, they cut their labourers' wages and then, as prices fell further, sacked men. Families were evicted from tied cottages and people starved. In an effort to stop prices falling further, the Corn Laws were passed to ban the importation of foreign grown cereals. Fearing political unrest, the authorities introduced measures to suppress 'seditious meetings'. *Habeus corpus*, the law which protect individuals from unlawful arrest, was suspended and the military were drafted in to keep order. Once armed soldiers were involved, it was only a matter of time before there would be a tragedy and, in 1819, soldiers killed fifteen demonstrators and injured up to 700 in Manchester in an event known as the 'Peterloo Massacre'.

Realising the difficulties facing his tenant farmers at Derry Ormond, John Jones decided to help, not by giving them charity but by finding them paid work to do. Jones decided to employ the men of the parish of Bettws Bledrws to build a tower and contacted Charles Robert Cockerell, a young architect, to ask his advice. Cockerell would eventually become one of the most prominent architects of his generation, responsible for designing many grand buildings across the land. Cockerell made some suggestions and passed the commission to Charles James of Llanddewi Brefi to design the tower John Jones wanted to build.

A local builder, David Morgan, whose gravestone in Bettws Bledrws churchyard states that he is 'the contractor and builder of the Derry Ormond Tower', employed local men to build the 127 feet (38.7 metres) tall tower. The site chosen for the tower was a hill on common land near Derry Ormond House and, when completed, the tower could be seen from miles away. Building the tower provided temporary relief but once it was finished there was no other employment for the men. Jones' solution was a radical one: he again asked his friend, the architect Cockerell for help. Cockerell designed a magnificent new country house for Jones, who then used a significant part of his fortune to build it. Once the new house was built, Jones demolished the country house that had been built by his grandfather a mere forty years before.

Having built what has been described as 'an elegant modern mansion in the neoclassical style', Jones continued spending his fortune. His next project was to landscape parkland around the mansion. Cockerell was given the task of designing the park and his scheme was ambitious, including, as it did, altering the course of the river below the house to create three lakes. When, in 1867, the Manchester and Milford Railway Company built a branch line between Carmarthen and Aberystwyth they added a small station at Derry Ormond Halt, illustrating the importance of the estate at that time. The passenger train service finished in 1964 and the line closed in 1970.

In the years following John Jones' major improvements to Derry Ormond and the building of his tower, the family fortune went into decline. In 1949, the owner, Wilmot Inglis-Jones – the family had changed its name – died, and in 1950 the mansion was sold for £3,000. It was demolished in 1953.

In the 1970s the tower was considered unsafe and it was suggested that it, too, should be demolished. One plan was for the army to blow it up. Fortunately, that act of vandalism was avoided and instead the army helped to reinforce the increasingly unstable structure with several tons of concrete.

By giving the men of Betws Bledrws work, John Jones may have alleviated their suffering, but it seems that by doing so he spent his family fortune, leaving the Derry Ormond Estate unable to support itself. No one knows for sure, but his folly has left one legacy: a tower that is now a listed building and serves no practical purpose except to intrigue those who see it.

35

Cilwendeg Shell House
Cardigan

When William Trench visited a group of islands off the coast of Anglesey (*Ynys Môn*) known as The Skerries (*Ynysoedd y Moelrhoniaid*) he came up with a money-making idea. The name Skerry derives from the Old Norse word 'sker', meaning small rock or reef. The position and rocky nature of the islands made them a hazard to passing ships and Trench's idea was to build a beacon to warn of the danger.

Trench started work on his lighthouse in 1716, and in 1724 he registered a patent to protect his idea. Shortly afterwards, Trench's son died in an accident at the lighthouse and within five years William himself was dead. The project he had hoped would make him rich had broken him, and he died penniless. Shipping tolls had proved to be an unreliable source of income. The dead man left nothing except one asset: his patent. The patent protecting the right to maintain a warning beacon on the Skerries passed to his son-in-law, Sutton Morgan.

Morgan was an astute fellow and petitioned for an Act of Parliament, allowing him to increase the charge levied on passing vessels. The Act was passed in 1730 when the rights he wanted were awarded to Morgan and his heirs in perpetuity. The lighthouse was improved and Morgan started to make money.

*Cilwendeg Shell House, paid for with income
from a lighthouse. Inside the shrine every surface
glistens with sea shells*

Morgan Jones, his son-in-law, inherited the lighthouse in 1779 and improved it again, raising the top and adding an oil-burning lamp in place of the previous coal brazier. At the same time, the amount of shipping passing Anglesey on its way to the docks at Liverpool was growing fast, and so too was the income produced by the lighthouse. The triangular slave trade between Liverpool, Africa and the New World was thriving and, because of their lighthouse revenue, the Jones family was becoming very wealthy.

By 1820, the next member of the family to own the lighthouse, another Morgan Jones, was earning more than £20,000 a year in income from the lighthouse (£1.5m in today's values). The family settled at

Boncath near Cardigan and were among the wealthiest in the county. The mansion they built, Cilwendeg Manor, included twenty-one bedrooms and every amenity that landed gentry might want. Having been granted the rights to the lighthouse revenue for ever, Morgan Jones was confident his family had a secure future.

Believing that he owed a debt of gratitude to his forebears, Morgan built a shrine to them and, in particular, to his immediate uncle, Morgan Jones Sr, in the form of a shell house. The uncle had been a quiet, rustic man of few words, and a bit of a recluse. As well as being a family shrine the shell house was designed to look like a hermit's cell while serving as a summer house and retreat, away from the grandeur of the mansion house. The folly was built deep in the woods, using local materials and decorated with shells, pieces of bone and coloured glass. Many of the shells originated in the West Indies, brought back by returning slave ships. In keeping with the prevailing fashion, the style of the building was Gothic and rather fanciful for a hermit's cell. Morgan Jones included a fireplace so the shell house could be used throughout the year.

Morgan Jones's good fortune was threatened when Trinity House, the official lighthouse authority, declared its intention to take over the Skerries lighthouse. Fearing the loss of the goose that kept laying him golden eggs, Morgan Jones put up a desperate fight, but an Act of Parliament enabling Trinity House to seize the lighthouse was passed in

1836. Trinity House took the lighthouse and Jones lost his franchise, together with the income he needed to maintain Cilwendeg Manor.

In 1952, Pembrokeshire Council bought Cilwendeg Manor and converted it into a care home, which it served as until 2010 when the home closed. The house was put up for sale in March 2012. One of the most prominent and stunning mansions in Wales was being returned to private ownership.

In the years since its construction, the shell house had deteriorated to the stage where it needed serious repairs in order to survive. In 2003 the Temple Trust, a historic building preservation trust, acquired the shell house and surrounding woods. The trust undertook a major restoration to return the folly to its original condition. Doing so revealed a strange but beautiful building that shimmers in the sunshine and captivates visitors who enter within to view the intricate shell patterns that decorate the walls. Today, the Temple Trust maintains the shell house and it is open to the public at certain times of the year.

36

The Arch
Cwmystwyth

Thomas Johnes Esq started life with all the advantages of wealth. Born near Ludlow, he was educated at Eton School, and at Edinburgh University, where he studied Greek, Latin and Moral Philosophy. After leaving Edinburgh, Johnes embarked on a grand tour of Europe, returning in 1771 to live as a country gentleman in Herefordshire. Within three years Johnes grew bored and embarked on a political career. In 1774 he was elected MP for Cardigan.

In 1780, Thomas Johnes inherited the Hafod Estate in Ceredigion. Hafod Urchtyd (*hafod*: summer place; *Uchrtyd*: personal name, possibly corresponding to the Old English name Oughtred) had once been a wealthy grange and part of vast lands owned by the monastery at Strata Florida (*Ystrad Fflur*). However, when Johnes arrived to take charge of the estate he found it in a poor condition. The property had been neglected. His tenants were living in squalor. Unable to scratch a living from the land, they were close to starving. The estate buildings were in ruins and there were no roads. No one was in charge. Despite the run down condition of his inheritance, Thomas Johnes was captivated by Hafod Urchtyd and fell in love with the beauty of

The Arch, Cwmystwyth

Cwmystwyth and the surrounding mountains. At last he had found a purpose, a project that would give his life meaning. He decided to restore Hafod Urchtyd to its former glory.

Johnes began by replacing his tenant's hovels with new cottages and employed the men to repair and rebuild the estate. He built a new church and took an active interest in his tenants' welfare. At the same time, the newly energised Johnes returned to his university studies. In 1783 he obtained an MA at Oxford University. In 1785 he built a new mansion at Hafod containing a magnificent library. Next to the library he constructed a conservatory that was 160 feet (49 metres) long and filled it with exotic plants. The walls of the mansion were covered with fine paintings and tapestries. Johnes employed designers to landscape a park in the 'Picturesque' style, to compliment his new mansion. He married in 1782 but his new bride fell ill and died shortly after. Quickly – some said indecently quickly – he was married again, to his cousin, and they had two children. Their son died in infancy and a daughter, Mariamne, with whom Johnes was besotted, was utterly spoiled.

Hafod Estate included 10,000 acres (40 square km) of barren upland. Here, Johnes embarked on a tree-planting campaign. Records show that between 1796 and 1801 more than 2 million trees were planted on the estate. The planting continued with Larch and Scots Pine on the high ground and Oak trees in the valleys. Each planting team was made up of one man and one boy, and was expected to plant 1,000 trees in a day. By the time Johnes finished planting his forests contained more than 3 million trees. In 1800 Johnes was elected a Fellow of the Royal Society. The reforestation of Hafod impressed the Royal Society of Arts so much they awarded him five gold medals between 1800 and 1810.

These were the best years for the estate. Jones was a practical landowner and eager to develop new ideas. He imported cattle from the Netherlands to improve the stock, experimented with new farming methods, and employed experts to train his workers.

Disaster struck in 1807 when Hafod House was gutted by fire, destroying everything. Fortunately the family was away at the time and no one was injured. The house took three years to rebuild. In 1810, wanting to celebrate the Golden Jubilee of King George III, Thomas Johnes built an arch across the road north-west of Cwmystwyth village. At the same time he built a free school for his tenants' children, started a sick fund and funded a doctor to tend to his tenants' needs. In addition to caring for his workers and developing the estate, Thomas Johnes built the Hafod Hotel, at Devil's Bridge (*Pontarfynach*), to encourage tourism in the area, and established the Hafod Press to publish his writings, which included books offering advice to his tenants, in both English and Welsh, and works he translated from French originals.

Each Christmas, Johnes and his wife entertained their tenants in their home. In addition to overseeing the management of his estate, Johnes continued a high-profile career as an MP and was Lord Lieutenant of Cardiganshire from 1800 until his death.

In 1811 Mariamne died. Her early death broke Johnes' heart. He never recovered from the loss of his beloved daughter. By 1814 Johnes was bankrupt, having spent his entire fortune on improving Hafod Uchrtyd. With deteriorating health and mentally broken, he moved to Langstone Cliff Cottage near Dawlish, Devon, where he died on 23 April 1816. Johnes' body was returned to Wales and interred at St Michael's Hafod church, the church he had earlier built for his tenants.

Following Johnes' death, the Hafod Estate changed hands several times and some of the land was sold. In 1958 the by then derelict Hafod Mansion was demolished. Today, most of the estate is owned by the Forestry Commission, who manages the woodland in partnership with Hafod Trust. Recently the partnership has created a series of walks for visitors to explore what is a very pretty part of Wales.

In November 2006, Cwmystwyth Arch, the folly built by Johnes, was damaged by a lorry trying to pass through it as it travelled along the B4574. Because of the structural damage the road had to be closed. Repairs were delayed while the owner of the arch was sought. Eventually, when no one admitted to owning the Grade II listed structure, Ceredigion Council in conjunction with Cadw were obliged to pay for the repairs. When the road initially reopened, traffic lights were used to control the flow, and vehicles limited to those under 11 feet tall. Since then, the road has been diverted around the folly to provide a more permanent (but in some ways controversial) solution. Nearby a car park and picnic area have been provided, and it is from here that three of the walks created by the Forestry Commission begin.

The road through Cwmystwyth has been described as one of the most enchanting in Wales and the folly arch built by Johnes has been called the gateway to the Elan Valley. Like other follies it's a pointless structure, but merits saving for posterity and is worth paying a visit.

37

Abereiddi Tower
St David's

The small hamlet of Abereiddi lies on the west coast of Pembrokeshire (*Sir Benfro*), north of St David's (*Tyddewi*). It's a hidden seaside gem that boasts a blue flag beach and ample parking for day trippers. At the north end of the beach is a lagoon and a headland known as Trwyncastell. The lagoon, whose water is stained blue by mineral deposits, was once a quarry. Slate was shipped from the quarry, along a 2-mile tramway, to waiting vessels at Porthgain. The quarry began to flood and was closed in the early part of the twentieth century. After slate mining finished, fishermen, who had previously dragged their boats up the beach, blasted a channel from the quarry to the sea and created a harbour.

According to Pembrokeshire National Park, the lagoon is 82 feet (25 metres) deep, making it suitable for a variety of water sports. In September 2012, divers from around the world used the lagoon for the Red Bull cliff diving competition. A diving board, 90 feet (27 metres) high, was suspended at the top of the cliff, and foolhardy individuals launched themselves at 90 miles per hour into the freezing water far below. The international competition returned to Abereiddi again in 2013.

Not far from where the diving board was placed

*Abereiddi Tower a navigation aid, watchtower,
gunpowder store or perhaps all three*

stands a small building known as Abereiddi Tower.

The stone tower is circular and has large windows
giving excellent views out to sea. No one is exactly
sure what the tower's purpose was, but a number of
suggestions have been made. One possibility is that
the tower was part of a fortification known to have
existed on the site, and was used as a lookout tower.
The name of the headland Trwyncastell suggests a
nose-shaped castle, adding strength to the suggestion.
Medieval coastal communities risked constant attack
from marauding pirates and a watch tower, to warn of
approaching vessels, would have been a wise precaution.

Another idea is that the tower was a navigation aid
to passing ships. In 1120, Pope Calistus II canonised
David and declared that two pilgrimages to St David's

tomb equalled one to Rome. Dewi Sant had become Saint David, the only Welsh saint recognised by the Catholic Church. St David's was an important shrine and pilgrims were travelling from across the known world to visit the holy place. Many arrived by sea, particularly from Ireland. The Pembrokeshire coastline was confusing and treacherous. Identifiable landmarks, such as Abereiddi Tower, told sailors where they were and served as a signpost for the voyage, much like modern-day lighthouses.

A more recent explanation for the tower is that the building was a gunpowder store for the slate quarry below the cliff. Explosives were highly dangerous and it made good sense to store them well away from anything else. The isolated position on the cliff was ideal. If there was an accident and the building blew up, its remoteness would limit any damage. Of the three suggestions, this is the most unlikely for two reasons. Anyone building a magazine would be unlikely to include large windows, and another building, without windows, exists near the beach, which is a more probable candidate for a gunpowder store.

Who built the Abereiddi Tower and why it was constructed will probably never be known for sure and it might have been used for all the above purposes at different times. One thing, however, is assured. Visitors to Abereiddi who climb the cliff path to see Trwyncastell will enjoy spectacular views of a beautiful coastline and discover a fascinating folly whose past is still a bit of a mystery.

38

Justinian's House
St David's

Walkers who travel along the Pembrokeshire coastal path through Porth Stinian (near St David's) pass close to a folly known as Justinian's House. The tiny pink house, which is circular, sits within the grounds of Justinian's bungalow, a modern luxury holiday home that can accommodate sixteen people. Slightly inland from the folly stand four walls, all that remains of a chapel where St Justinian was buried. According to legend, St Justinian was a sixth-century Breton nobleman who gave away his wealth and moved to Ramsey Island (*Ynys Dewi*) to live as a hermit. Hearing of his new neighbour, St David walked to Porth Stinian and told the ferryman to row him to the island. Having met Justinian, David was impressed by the hermit's devotion and godliness. David persuaded Justinian to return with him to be the abbot of St David's cathedral and become David's confessor.

At first, Justinian was happy at the cathedral but, as time passed, he grew weary of his new role. The monks at St David's were lazy and lacked moral fibre. Justinian became disenchanted and returned to Ramsey Island. Monks who had grown fond of Justinian followed him and together they established a new religious community on the island. Justinian

St Justinian's House was more likely to have been used by the ferryman than the saint

expected his followers to rise before the sun came up and spend the day praying. Before long the monks started to complain that he was too strict. To escape the moaning, Justinian would retreat to the mainland where he built a chapel.

Near the chapel, he added a small house to stay in when the monks on the island got on his nerves.

During one of Justinian's retreats from Ramsey Island, the monks plotted against him and when the saint returned they murdered him and cut off his head. What happened next shocked the murderers. The headless Justinian stood up, tucked his head under his arm and walked across the sea to his chapel at Porth Stinian, where he lay down. He was buried there.

It's an entertaining legend, and the remains of the

chapel at Porth Stinian, together with the little house nearby, add to the telling. If Justinian walked to the mainland, it would have been a miracle even with his head in place. The stretch of sea between Ramsey Island and the mainland is particularly dangerous with strong rip tides and a series of rocks named 'The Bitches' lying half submerged at different times. Recognising the danger of the waters around Ramsey, a lifeboat was stationed at Porth Stinian in 1869. Since then, the lifeboat has saved more than 360 lives and won recognition for the bravery of its crews, some of whom sacrificed their own lives saving others.

Whether the legend is true or false, St Justinian is included in the ancient Welsh calendar of saints and martyrs. After he was made a saint, his remains were exhumed and the bones removed to St David's cathedral to be placed in a casket in the Holy Trinity chapel. Unfortunately, carbon dating of the bones dates them to the twelfth century, 600 years after the saint's death.

The folly was made a Grade II listed building in 1962 and St Justinian's chapel was added to the list in 1963.

Although the chapel at Porth Stinian may have a connection to St Justinian, the folly almost certainly does not. It was built later, possibly as a lookout tower or a dwelling for the ferryman who rowed passengers between Ramsey Island and the mainland.

39

The Malakoff
St Ishmael

Walk west along the Pembrokeshire Coastal Path from Monk Haven, near St Ishmael (*Llanismel*), and you will discover a small tower, known as the Malakoff, on a headland called Watch Tower Point. Nearby are gun positions built in the twentieth century to protect Milford Haven from attack by enemy ships and aircraft. The defensive importance of the point near the mouth of the Haven is apparent and one might mistakenly assume that the Malakoff tower had a similar function, as a look-out point. Although the tower's name derives from a conflict that took place at the eastern end of the Mediterranean, the Malakoff Tower at Monk Haven never had a military use.

The Crimean War started in October 1853 and lasted until February 1856. It was a brutal conflict between the Russian Empire and an alliance of France, Britain, Ottoman and Sardinian forces. The war began with a religious dispute between Russia and the Ottoman Empire and quickly escalated into military action which claimed more than 500,000 lives. In September 1854, allied forces landed north of Sebastopol. It took them a year of fighting to travel 35 miles (56 km) along the coast and take the city. The Russian Black Sea Fleet was based at Sebastopol,

*Malakoff Tower named after an important battle
during the Crimean War*

which Tsar Nicholas I had determined to hold regardless of the cost in human life. Russian ships were scuttled in the mouth of the harbour and the sailors sent to man the defences.

At the beginning of the war the Russians had begun to build a line of defensive forts, known as Malakoff forts, along a prominent ridge to protect the city. The granite bastions were well armed with artillery and inflicted heavy casualties on the allies. In return, the French and British fleets shelled the city, while siege guns were dragged forward to intensify the bombardment. Months passed as the artillery duel slowly wore down the Russian defences. The defenders were dying at the rate of 250 a day. Eventually, allied commanders agreed that it was time to launch an attack and capture the Malakoff Forts. For the attack to succeed the allies needed to overcome a Russian command position called Malakoff Kurgan. The Malakoff Kurgan was a fortification 49 feet (15 metres) in diameter and 26 feet (8 metres) tall, flanked by two forts able to threaten crossfire. It would be difficult to take.

The final assault started at midday on 8 September 1855. An entire French corps scaled the Malakoff while British forces attacked the other forts. Fighting was hand to hand and every inch paid for in blood. By nightfall the Russians had had enough and withdrew leaving the burning city to the allies. The French succeeded in taking the Malakoff Kurgan while the British attack on the other positions failed. A painting by Horace Vernet shows the French flag flying proudly above the ruined fortress, being saluted by an English officer. Ten thousand allied soldiers perished in the battle, and 13,000 Russians fell trying to defend Sebastopol. The action at Malakoff was the decisive battle of the Crimean War and an armistice was signed the following February.

After the Crimean War, towers across Europe were renamed Malakoff. A cake was named after the Duke of Malakoff, a Swiss cheese dish became known as Malakoff and a suburb of Paris was given the name Malakoff. At Monk Haven, the owner of Trewarren Estate had recently built a modest cliff top folly to use for picnics and afternoons out. To celebrate the allies' victory against the Russians, he named it Malakoff Tower.

The Monk Haven Malakoff Tower was never used by the military, but the Malakoff Kurgan saw action again during 1942 when it was stormed by Nazi troops. Today, a flame burns near the top of the Malakoff Kurgan, above the grave of an unknown Russian sailor, in honour of all the men that died defending Sebastopol.

40

Palmerston's Follies
Pembrokeshire

Milford Haven (*Aberdaugleddau*) was described by Admiral Lord Nelson as 'the finest port in Christendom', and for this reason the Royal Navy chose the natural harbour as a site for one of its dockyards. Visit the Haven today and you will find a series of Victorian forts and gun emplacements. The forts are known as 'Palmerston's Follies'. Several forts were built to provide interlocking artillery fire designed to defend Pembroke Dock (*Doc Penfro*) from enemy attack. The reason they became known as follies is an interesting story.

In 1859, Henry John Temple, 3rd Viscount Palmerston, was returned to office as Prime Minister for a second time. Palmerston had been educated at Eton and Edinburgh, could speak and write fluent Italian and had been in almost continuous political office for over fifty years. In the nineteenth century the British Empire was at the height of its power, Queen Victoria was on the throne and Lord Palmerston, like many of his peers, regarded British supremacy as a natural condition. Palmerston was a powerful orator but inclined to be abrasive and combative with his opponents, earning him the nickname 'Lord Pumice stone'. In matters of foreign affairs he was often belligerent and inclined to employ gunboat diplomacy.

Palmerston folly, just one of the tower he built to defend against a French invasion that never came

One of the first orders of business, after Palmerston's return to office, was to set up a 'Royal Commission on the Defence of the United Kingdom'. The commission completed its report in 1860. At the time, there were serious concerns that France was building up its navy and, in consequence, there was a likelihood of invasion in the event of a war with the old enemy. To combat this threat, the Royal Commission recommended that naval dockyards should be protected by a series of forts.

During the Napoleonic wars, sixty years earlier, a series of over 100 fortifications had been built to protect major dockyards, but these Martello Towers, as they were known, were no longer considered adequate for the job. In the intervening years, gunnery and naval firepower had made major advances. ('Martello' is a misspelling of the name 'Mortella', which is a point on the coast of Corsica, where a Genovese defence system known as Terra d'Mortella existed.)

Palmerston decided to implement the recommendations of the Royal Commission but there was a problem: to build the fortification would be enormously expensive. Work started almost immediately and as the forts were constructed around the country questions began to be asked concerning where the money was coming from to pay for the building work. Britain's finances were already in dire straits and income tax at 5 old pence (2p) in the pound had been introduced. The Chancellor of the Exchequer, William Gladstone, objected to the cost of the scheme and sent several letters threatening to resign, causing Palmerston to comment: 'I have so many resignation letters from Gladstone that I fear they will set fire to the chimney'.

As the building work progressed, costs began to rise and Gladstone was forced to raise more money by increasing income tax to 9 old pence (3.5p). Increasing taxation was not enough and the government began to borrow money to fund the project. It was now that the forts came to be known as 'Palmerston's Follies', but it was not because of the exorbitant cost. The reason was that some of the gun positions faced inland, away from any expected seaborne invasion. People sneered at the forts, unaware that the guns faced inland for a very good reason: to protect the naval dockyards from French forces that might land elsewhere and attack overland. It was a strategy that the Japanese later used with devastating effect when they took Singapore in 1942 and captured 80,000 allied prisoners of war, many of whom died in captivity. Singapore's main defences, naval 15-inch guns firing high explosive shells, were positioned to destroy enemy shipping: the Japanese attacked overland, taking Singapore from the rear.

In 1865 Lord Palmerston died, but his programme of constructing defensive forts continued. Then, in 1870, a war between France and Prussia broke out in which the Prussian army was victorious. The defeat created an anti-war atmosphere in France and significantly changed the politics of Europe. There was no longer any danger of an invasion from France. Instead, a new threat had emerged from a warlike Prussia, led by Bismark (known as 'The Iron Chancellor'), which was now reunited with the rest of Germany.

The cost of Palmerston's fort building programme continued to grow. In 1890, Members of Parliament demanded to know the true cost. It was revealed that over £12m had been spent on the forts, £5.5m had been spent purchasing the cannons to arm them and a further £3m to provide accommodation for the garrisons that would be needed. Using wage inflation as a guide, in today's values Palmerston's forts had cost £12.2 billion and many were never finished.

The forts Palmerston built to protect Milford Haven and its Royal Naval Dockyard included Fort

Hubberstone, Popton Fort, Scoveston Fort, South Hook Fort, South Roch Fort and Thorn Island Fort. In total, something like eighty-five forts were built as a result of Palmerston's ambitious plan and it was the most expensive defensive building project ever undertaken in the British Isles. Today, there is a Palmerston Forts Society, whose members have regular meetings and share their interest in Victorian fortifications.

41

Orielton Banqueting Tower
Pembrokeshire

Once a grand three-storey building, Orielton Banqueting Tower now stands alone and neglected in the south-western corner of Wales. The tower's gaily decorated rooms, bright fireplaces and fancy ceilings were abandoned more than 100 years ago. Since then, nature has reclaimed it. The roof collapsed long ago and, exposed to the elements, the tower is now a decaying ruin. The baronet John Owen built the tower in about 1850 but within a few years it was locked, never to be used again.

In 1571, Sir Hugh Owen married Elizabeth Wirriot, heiress to a fortune. Her dowry included properties in Pembroke (*Penfro*) and the Orielton Estate, south-west of the busy seaport. Sir Hugh came from an ancient Welsh family with estates on Anglesey, and was a wealthy man. The Owens were a prominent family and Sir Hugh, a lawyer, served as the Sheriff of Pembrokeshire. When he died his Pembrokeshire estates passed to his grandson, also Hugh Owen, who was Sheriff of Pembrokeshire from 1634 to 1654. He was made a baronet in 1641, the same year the 'English' civil war began.

During the ten-year war Sir Hugh Owen astutely vacillated between sides, intent on keeping his

*John Owen's planned to entertain in the tower
but was bankrupted before it was completed*

family's fortune intact. At the start of the war, Owen supported parliament but changed his allegiance in favour of the king. When the tide of war turned against King Charles, the opportunistic Owen changed sides again. His strategy worked and his position in society was secured.

Generations of Owens were involved in the political life of the county. Pembroke was controlled by a council whose members were elected for life by the merchants. The councillors worked closely with the Owen family, who owned much of the town. It was a cosy relationship. Owen family members were also elected to parliament. One such MP was Sir Arthur Owen. It was Sir Arthur who, in 1702, famously galloped to London to give the casting vote for the Act of Settlement, securing the Hanoverian right of succession to the throne.

At the time, parliamentary candidates bought votes, and gerrymandering – the manipulation of constituencies to influence electoral results – was commonplace. Bribery and violence often replaced reasoning and debate. During one election, when there was a particularly strong challenge for his seat, Sir Arthur Owen employed thugs to break up his opponents' meetings. Despite the intimidation Sir Arthur was defeated by a landslide. The returning officer, however, was in Arthur Owen's employ and, ignoring the result, declared Sir Arthur the winner. The family motto 'Honesty is the best policy' did not, apparently, apply to politics. The result of the election was later overturned on appeal to parliament.

In 1786, the 6th Baronet, another Hugh, inherited. He was four years old. The young baronet died unmarried and childless in 1809. He was twenty-seven. When he died, the title passed to another male member of the family – but the will bequeathed all the young baronet's possessions to John Lord, a distant cousin. John Lord was an impulsive man who, in 1800, had eloped to Gretna Green with Charlotte Phillips, only to discover that her family was not wealthy.

The new owner of Orielton promptly changed his name to Owen, and in 1813 a second Owen Baronetcy of Orielton was created for his benefit. There were now two men with the title 'Owen Baronet Orielton'. The new baronet, Sir John Owen began a campaign to become a Member of Parliament. Several fiercely fought and very dirty elections followed on which John Owen spent a great deal of money. Sir John committed numerous electoral irregularities and, in 1831, was finally elected. His opponent petitioned Parliament with evidence of vote-rigging and the election was declared void. A new election was held and an unrepentant Owen was again returned as the MP with an even larger majority.

As well as spending his money on winning elections, the Member of Parliament for Pembroke enjoyed a lavish lifestyle. One thing he decided he needed was a banqueting tower. It was to be an elegant building with an archway for carriages to pass through on the ground floor. Stairs led to the upper floors containing reception and dining rooms.

The money ran out in 1857 while the banqueting tower was being built. John Owen was bankrupt. One man's profligacy had squandered the family fortune. Orielton Estate was put up for sale and the properties in Pembroke were auctioned off to pay creditors.

John Owen died in 1861. Both titles 'Owen, Baronet Orielton' have since become extinct.

In the early 1950s the house was bought by R. M. Lockley, the well-known naturalist and ornithologist, for £5,000. In 1963, the Georgian mansion at Orielton became a Field Studies Centre, offering outdoor learning for schools, professional development for teachers, individuals and families. The folly, standing south west of the centre, continues to decay. No one, it seems, has a use for a 160-year-old banqueting tower without a roof.

42

The Dolwilym Arch
Llanglydwen

A strange stone arch sits astride the lane leading to St Cledwyn's Church. The church stands on a hill overlooking the River Taf and below it nestles the village of Llanglydwen. Ancient legends tell that St Cledwyn was the son of King Brychan of Brycheiniog who, as well as carrying out his kingly duties, sired forty children. Cledwyn was a warrior saint and the site of the church, the only one consecrated in his name, was once fortified for defence. The graveyard is circular, perhaps because of earlier ramparts, although another reason might have been to make it difficult for demons and evil spirits to hide in corners. Many ancient graveyards were circular because of such beliefs.

A Celtic cross in the graveyard is believed to have been carved around the eighth century but there was a church here in much earlier times. In 1594 a yeoman farmer by the name Rhydderch ap John ap Rhys purchased Dolwilym Estate. His new lands came complete with the church. His son, Evan ap Rhydderch (Evan son of Rhydderch), turned from the Welsh way of using his father's Christian name to describe himself and adopted the surname Prydderch, which soon became anglicized as Protheroe. The last male Protheroe, another Evan, died in 1785 aged

Dolwilym Arch once led to a grand house

eighty, leaving the estate to his brother-in-law, Dr Jones from Carmarthen. The will stipulated that, in order to inherit, the doctor was required to change his name to Protheroe, which he duly did. When the doctor passed away his daughter and her husband moved in and continued to use the surname Protheroe, although their married name was Schaw.

A new mansion was built on the estate in 1845 and rebuilt again in 1908 following a fire. During the First World War Dolwilym was used as a German prisoner-of-war camp. When it was returned to private use the house was in a dilapidated state. It continued to deteriorate and the Protheroe family continued to live at a property in nearby Glyntaf. By then, the Protheroes had fallen on hard times. Dolwilym House was stripped for salvage and subsequently sold in the 1960s.

The new owner, Giles Chaplin, used the estate for a variety of things including a hippie commune, an antiques business, theatre and recording studios. The main house, which had become an unsafe shell, was demolished in 1986.

Exactly when and why Dolwilym Arch was built is unclear but it is believed that it was constructed by the Protheroes as a memorial to a family member killed in the 1914–1918 war. The archway was recorded as a lychgate and made a listed building in 1999. It's a strange Gothic structure with crenellated towers on either side but, with no means of access, the battlements and the arch serve no purpose other than as decoration. Examination of the inside of the uprights suggests gates once hung within the arch but these no longer exist. Today, as well as giving access to St Cledwyn's Church, Dolwilym Arch is the portal leading to holiday cottages, an antique centre and recording studios built in the grounds of the old house.

43

The Picton Obelisk
Carmarthen

Thomas Picton was born in Haverfordwest (*Hwlffordd*), Pembrokshire, in 1758 and began a military career in 1771 as an ensign serving in the 12th Regiment of Foot. During a posting to Gibraltar he gained promotion to the rank of captain. The regiment returned to Britain and, in 1883, its disbandment was announced. Hearing the news, the men mutinied. Picton intervened and as a result of his immediate, forceful action the mutiny was squashed. Now jobless, he spent the next twelve years living as a retired officer on his father's estate until he was offered a post in the West Indies. Captain Picton became aide-de-camp to Sir John Vaughn, the Garrison Commander. Arriving in the Caribbean, Picton quickly proved his leadership ability and steady promotion followed.

In February 1797 a British squadron seized Trinidad from the Spanish and Picton, by now a lieutenant colonel, was appointed governor of the island, a post he held for the next five years. His garrison was undermanned and there was a constant threat of rebellion by slaves or disgruntled Spaniards still living on the island. Picton's response was brutal. He ordered the use of torture, and suspects were summarily executed. The policy the governor used to

Picton's Obelisk commemorates the most senior British officer killed at the Battle of Waterloo

control the island's population was succinctly described by William Fullarton, a commissioner on the island, 'Let them hate so long as they fear'. Fullarton would later be instrumental in having Picton prosecuted as a result of his harsh treatment.

Not all of the governor's actions were designed to maintain control of the island. Picton had taken a mulatto mistress who is said to have used her position of influence to settle old scores. As well as terrorising the islanders, Picton used his position to profit from the sale of land and slaves. Eventually word of his despotism reached the UK and in 1803 Picton returned to face arrest for charges levelled against him by Fullarton. Picton was released with bail set at £40,000. During his trial before the Privy Council Picton argued that the island of Trinidad was still technically being governed according to Spanish law, and according to that law he was well within his rights to use torture and summary execution. It was a dubious argument, but when he added that the state of unrest on the island and its garrison's weakness made such action necessary, the charges were dropped.

That, however, was not the end of the matter. A lower court took up the case of Luisa, a free 14-year-old servant girl Picton had ordered to be tortured. The girl was accused of helping in the burglary of her employer's house. The torture involved being partially stripped, suspended by her thumbs and made to stand on her toes on the flat end of a peg driven into the ground. The torture lasted for one hour at a time. During it the poor girl had the stark choice of taking her weight on her thumbs and dislocating them or putting her weight on her toes. Similar military punishments, known as 'piqueting', were used in medieval times. Salacious engravings of the torture, referred to as 'Pictoning' and published in the press, excited public interest and the case became a cause célèbre. Once again, Picton used the defence that Spanish law permits the torture of suspects; he was found guilty and demanded a retrial.

Military friends and wealthy plantation owners provided funds to fight the case and, although the jury's verdict was overruled, no final decision was made regarding the legality of Spanish law as a defence in such cases. It made no difference. Picton was presented at the trial as a hero defending British interests. His popularity soared and he was promoted to the rank of Major General.

In 1810 Picton joined Wellington's army as a divisional commander and remained one of

Wellington's senior officers throughout the Peninsular War. By now, Picton had developed a reputation as a competent but ruthless soldier. The historian Allesandro Barbero described Picton as 'respected for his courage and feared for his irascible temperament'. Picton was frequently in the thick of the action and led from the front. During the Battle of Badajoz, Picton led his men, known as the Fighting 3rd Division, in an attack and captured an enemy fortress. As he scaled the walls, the general was wounded. Despite his wounds the general remained in charge of the situation and held the fort when the enemy tried to retake it. Returning home to recuperate, the Prince Regent invested Picton as a Knight of the Order of the Bath. At the Battle of Vitoria, Picton led his division and captured an important bridge. Despite a ferocious enemy counter attack and withering cannon fire, Picton held the bridge. Doing so cost the lives of 1,800 of his men. The Fighting 3rd Division had many admirers, and Picton received the thanks of parliament on seven different occasions. He had grown to be a revered and celebrated figure in the army. Not everyone was so appreciative; Picton's men resented him because of his willingness to sacrifice soldiers' lives. Picton was wounded again at Quatre Bras. The damage to his hip made him walk with a peculiar gait. Fearing that he would be retired and sent home, the general concealed the injury to everyone except his valet.

On 18 June 1815 Wellington's allied army engaged the French army commanded by Napoleon Bonaparte near a small village in Belgium. The Battle of Waterloo was, according to the Wellington's own account, 'The nearest run thing you ever saw in your life'. The battle which lasted all day started with 136,000 men in the field.

During the morning an artillery officer named Mercer was bringing his cannons into action when he was engaged in conversation by a shabby-looking man dressed in civilian clothes and wearing a rather odd-looking hat. The man, who walked with a limp, enquired how the day was going and, assuming him to be a sightseer – there were uninvited spectators on the battlefield – Mercer was curt in his replies. The man Mercer was abrupt to was General Picton. The general had just arrived from England and, having lost his baggage, had no uniform to wear. Receiving short shift from the artillery officer, Picton wandered off to look for his division.

Later in the morning, Picton assumed his command, still dressed in civilian clothes, and led a bayonet charge, halting a French attack. Picton's hat was shot off by a cannon ball but the hatless general did not pause and urged his men to press home their assault. As he encouraged his men forward, a musket ball passed through his temple and killed him. It is unclear who killed Picton and it has been suggested by some commentators that he was shot from behind by one of his own men. There is no historical evidence to support the assertion but it is not unknown for old scores to be settled in the chaos of battle. Lieutenant General Sir Thomas Picton KCB was the most senior

British officer to die at Waterloo. He was fifty-six years old.

Fierce fighting continued between the evenly-matched armies until late afternoon when the morale of the French suddenly collapsed and they quickly turned into a rabble. What remained of the French army fled leaving a battlefield strewn with 47,000 corpses.

Picton's death at Waterloo made him an international hero. Towns were named after him in New Zealand, Canada and Australia. Roads were named after the fallen hero. The navy commissioned *HMS Sir Thomas Picton* in his honour, and the army named a barracks after the dead general. Parliament ordered that a monument be erected in St Paul's Cathedral. In Wales, schools, taverns and coaching inns and were renamed, and in Carmarthen (*Caerfyrddin*) a fund was launched to build a monument to remember the famous Welshman. The king contributed 100 guineas to the fund and a large obelisk was erected at the western end of the town. The 75-foot tall monument, modelled on Trajan's column in Rome, was finished in 1828. Reliefs depicting Picton's military actions were carved around the plinth. The top of the square tower supported a platform with cannons at each corner and a statue of the general.

Within a few years the obelisk was in a dilapidated state. Inclement weather had badly damaged the base reliefs. The original stonemason, Edward Hodges Baily, was commissioned to carve replacements but before they could be fitted the monument was declared unsafe and, in 1846, was dismantled. New heavier foundations were laid and the obelisk was re-erected the following year without the replacement sculptures. Baily's new carvings were abandoned in a Johnstown yard until they were rediscovered in the 1970s and moved to the museum in Carmarthen. In 1984, concerns were again raised about the monument's safety, resulting in it being taken down yet again and rebuilt stone by stone.

Today the monument is a plain obelisk. The statue of Lieutenant General Sir Thomas Picton and the four cannons have gone. Even without these adornments the obelisk remains an imposing memorial to a ruthless hero, capable of being both brave and cruel.

44

Paxton's Tower
Llandeilo

There is a strange-looking Gothic tower standing high above the Tywi valley between Carmarthen and Llandeilo which was built by a Scotsman – according to some, to snub the people of Carmarthenshire. William Paxton was born in Edinburgh in 1745. He joined the Royal Navy as a young man but, on arrival in India, realised that the new colony was a place of adventure and a land of opportunity. This was the place for an ambitious young fellow to make his fortune. Seizing his chance, Paxton resigned from the navy and became a banker. He had a sharp mind and quickly won promotion. Within a few years he became the Master of the Calcutta Mint and, like other nabobs of the time, amassed a huge fortune for himself.

In 1785 Paxton returned from India rich, and intent on becoming a country gentleman. He purchased Middleton Hall, a run-down estate in the Tywi valley, and started to improve it. Samuel Peyps Cockerell, a leading architect of the day, was commissioned to design a new country house. A country park was laid out and the house, described as the most perfect in the country, was completed in 1795.

Paxton was intent on winning respectability and used his great wealth to demonstrate his importance. Despite his grandeur, he had difficulty becoming

Paxton's Tower, built by a nabob after losing an election

accepted. The noble families, comfortable with their old money, were snobbish and thought him conceited and vulgar. The poor were afraid of him and distrusted him.

Despite his unpopularity, Paxton saw politics as a means to fulfil his ambition. He knew that his money and patronage would create the support he needed. These were the days of rotten boroughs, when votes were bought and bribery common. Paxton used his money to good effect and was soon knighted. Local elections took place and Paxton was elected Mayor of Carmarthen. In this capacity he entertained Admiral Lord Nelson, who was visiting the town.

Paxton soon realised that local politics would not satisfy his aspirations. He wanted a bigger stage to perform on and decided to stand for parliament. He started campaigning during the 1802 general election, spending money to win votes. He made promises and bought beer for the voters. One particular pledge made by Paxton was that, if elected, he would pay for a bridge over the Tywi. Despite his grand promises and a vast sum spent on bribes, the voters rejected Paxton and he failed to win the seat.

The reason Paxton failed to get elected was that someone, possibly his opponent, had started a rumour that he was insolvent and unfit to represent the people in Parliament. Determined to prove that the rumour was a lie, but unwilling to build a bridge for the ungrateful electors, Paxton chose instead to spend the £15,000 that the bridge would have cost on a tower to celebrate the victories of Admiral Nelson.

It was to be a sweet and very prominent revenge. The architect Cockerell was summoned and a suitable site selected high on Bryn y Bigwrn Hill. Cockerell proposed a 500-foot tall Gothic-style structure that would dominate the countryside. Work began using limestone quarried locally, and the Scottish stonemasons that he employed gave the tower a character that reminded Paxton of his birthplace, Edinburgh.

Apart from making a statement to the people of Carmarthenshire, the tower had a second purpose. It was designed so that carriages could arrive from Middleton Hall and drive inside the three-cornered base, allowing passengers to alight in the dry and to climb up stairways to a grand dining room with superb views over the Tywi valley. It was here that

Paxton entertained his guests and impressed his visitors. From the top of the tower you could see seven different counties. The walls of the rooms were clad in marble and there were three fabulous stained glass windows depicting Lord Nelson, his victories and his heroic death at Trafalgar. (Nelson had died in 1805, six years before the tower was completed.)

If the tower was a snub, the people failed to understand its meaning, and Paxton succeeded in winning election to Westminster at his second attempt in 1806. He lived to the age of eighty, passing away in 1824. The estate was put up for sale the same year and the catalogue described the tower thus:

A Gothic Tower, Erected by the late liberal-minded Possessor, in Commemoration of our Noble Hero, Lord Nelson; A grand Ornament and Land Mark in the County. On the Ground Floor, Three Spacious Lofty Arches for the Admission of Carriages, On the Principal Story, A Banqueting Room, with Gothic Ceiling; A Boudoir and Closet, over which A Prospect Room or Observatory, with Turrets, Three of the Windows are fitted with Stained Glass, One Window representing his Lordship, the others emblematical of his Fate, From which there is a Panoramic View, of a grandeur and extent that may justly be said to stand unrivalled. On the upper Part a Lead Flat, and Two Entrance Lodges.

William Paxton never did build the bridge across the Tywi.

45

Mail Coach Monument
Sennybridge–Llandovery Road

The road that we now call the A40 has for centuries been a main transport route across Wales. In Roman times, it was a military road that linked the garrison towns like Brecon (*Aberhonddu*) and Carmarthen to enable the fast movement of troop reinforcements between different points. After the Romans withdrew, the roads deteriorated and the main route along the Tywi valley was no exception. Travellers wishing to cross the country used other ancient byways made passable by drovers, who were moving livestock from the farms of Wales to the more lucrative markets of England. It was not until the Turnpike Trusts, which came into being in the eighteenth century, that things began to improve, and fast mail services, using horse-drawn stagecoaches, would again connect distant towns along well-kept roads.

Tolls were charged to pay for the roads, some of which amounted to extortion. This led to a rebellion between 1839 and 1843 known as the Rebecca Riots, as farmers and agricultural workers objected, sometimes violently, to being charged large amounts to move their farm vehicles and stock. The toll-gates were seen as a manifestation of taxation. The protesters would dress up as women – 'Rebecca's Daughters' – and by night would set fire to gates and toll-houses.

The Mail Coach Monument
proving that drunken driving
is not a new phenomena

Part of the inscription
recording the details
of the accident

Despite the inequities of overcharging, turnpikes remained the model for road building for over 100 years.

In the eighteenth century, stagecoach travel could be dangerous. To make more money, coaches were overloaded, sometimes with up to eighteen passengers, some of whom travelled, precariously, on the top of the coach. Falling asleep was dangerous – hence the term 'dropping off'. Highwaymen were another threat and stagecoaches carried a guard armed with a blunderbuss, an inaccurate weapon often loaded with an assortment of bits of metal and other shrapnel.

Coaches would race between 10 and 15 miles to complete each 'stage' before changing the sweating horses for a new team, ready for the next stage of the journey. As the stagecoach approached the end of a stage, the guard would blow a horn to clear the road ahead and warn that a new team of horses was needed or that there were passengers requiring accommodation for the night. Ostlers, as the stablemen were known, could change a team of horses in less than a minute and the bigger coaching inns, which specialised in servicing stagecoaches, would have more than fifty horses in their stables. As the quality of the roads improved, the stagecoaches got faster, and, with average speeds approaching 10 miles per hour, they ran to regular timetables.

On 19 December 1835, Edward Jenkins was driving his Gloucester to Carmarthen Royal Mail coach west, along the turnpike between Sennybridge (*Pontsenni*) and Llandovery (*Llanymddyfri*). The coach was lightly loaded and Jenkins had whipped up the horses to a full gallop as they approached a left-hand bend. The team of horses drifted across the road as they began to turn – only to find they were heading directly towards a cart coming in the opposite direction. Jenkins, who had been drinking, tried to turn the team to the left but he lost control, whereupon the horses charged off the road and down a 121-foot (38 metre) precipice, dragging the coach and its occupants with them.

When it reached the bottom of the precipice, the coach hit a large ash tree and disintegrated, scattering the coachman, guard and passengers across the bottom of the ravine. Passengers on the outside included a Colonel Gwynn, Daniel Jones and a Mr Edwards. Those who had paid more for their tickets and started the journey inside were David Lloyd Harris, a Llandovery solicitor, and a young lad believed to be called Kernick.

Miraculously, all the people on the coach survived the accident. Following the crash, the coachman, Jenkins, was fined £5 plus costs by the magistrate at Llandovery for being inebriated while in charge of a mail coach. He always denied being drunk at the time of the accident.

In 1841, six years after the accident, a monument was erected at the point where the stagecoach left the road. It's a modest obelisk surrounded by a cast metal fence which today looks as if it has been left as an obstruction in the middle of a lay-by. The monument bears the following inscription:

This pillar is called mail coach pillar and erected as a caution to keep from intoxication and in memory of the Gloucester & Carmarthen Mail Coach which was driven by Edward Jenkins on the 19th Day of December in the year 1835, who was intoxicated at the time & drove the mail on the wrong side of the road and going at full speed or gallop met a cart & permitted the leader to turn short round to the right and went down over the precipice 121 feet where at the bottom near the river it came against an ash tree when the coach was dashed into several pieces. Colonel Gwynn of Glan Brian Park, Daniel Jones Esq of Penybont & a person of the name of Edwards were outside & David Lloyd Harris Esq of Llandovery Solicitor and a lad of the name Kernick were inside passengers by the mail at the time and John Compton outside. I have heard say where there is a will there is a way one person cannot assist many, but many can assist a few as this pillar will shew which was suggested designed and erected by J. Bull Inspector of Mail Coaches, with the aid of thirteen pounds sixteen shillings and six pence received by him from fortyone subscribers in the year 1841. The work of this pillar was executed by John Jones Marble and Stone Mason Llanddarog near Carmarthen.

REPAINTED AND RESTORED BY POSTAL OFFICIALS 1930

Sadly the condition of the pillar has deteriorated since it was restored in 1930. The top has been broken off, probably by a commercial vehicle reversing into it, and the railings are shabby. At the time of writing there are plans in place to restore the monument so that it will continue to serve as a reminder to avoid drinking and driving, a warning that is as relevant today as it was in 1835.

46

Davies' Stone
Llangadog–Brynaman Road

The A4069 is a narrow country road that snakes its way over the Black Mountain from Llangadog to Brynaman. A good surface, hairpin bends and stunning views make the road a popular location for film crews trying to make fast cars look exciting. On sunny weekends, hordes of motorcyclists gather at the West End café in Llandovery (*Llanymddyfri*) before roaring over the mountain in a cavalcade of noise. Most thunder by the disused quarries without seeing them, and fail to notice the strange upright stone marker on a mound near the road.

More sedate travellers wonder why the stone marker was put up on such a lonely mountain pass but soon forget it as they go on their way. Today, the mountain is in a National Park. Sheep graze on the slopes while tourists stop to picnic, take photographs and enjoy the clean air. Years ago, the scene was far from tranquil; the Black Mountain (*Mynydd Du*) was an industrial landscape.

In the twelfth century, farmers gathered limestone rocks from the mountain and stacked them in freshly-dug pits. They covered the limestone with gorse, ferns and timber to build a large fire. Once the fire was lit it was sealed with earth to keep in the heat. The clamp kilns, as they were known, had to reach over 900 °C to

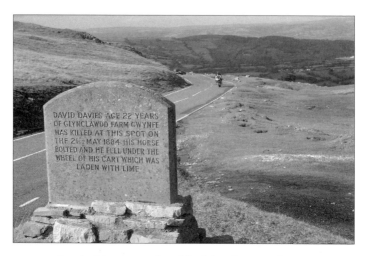

Davies' Stone, replaced by his relatives in 1987

Herbert's Quarry, the ruined weigh office is in the foreground while Davies' Stone lies beyond

create what the farmers were after – lime. After the kilns had cooled, they were opened and the lime spread on the land, where it neutralised acidity and increased yields, particularly on poor-quality upland fields. Medieval Welsh manuscripts describe how to make clamp kilns and instruct the user to 'Bestow lime once in nine years upon arable land and once in 18 years upon grassland'.

The remains of clamp kilns can still be seen on the north side of the mountain. Before long, other uses were found for lime. It was caustic and ideal for speeding up decomposition of dead and often diseased bodies. The new industry of glass-making needed lime to mix with sodium carbonate and silica sand. Lime was used for making soap, plaster, mortar and lime-wash paints. Limestone was needed as a flux to smelt copper and iron. Calcium oxide, a lime product, was used to create a bright white light for theatre productions, hence the expression 'In the limelight'. What had started as a small local enterprise expanded. Use of Black Mountain limestone grew from a few farmers improving their land to a major industry. Quarries got bigger, dirtier and more dangerous. Flare and draw kilns, which were larger and more efficient, replaced the clamp kilns.

Gangs of quarrymen trudged up the mountain on Sunday nights ready for the week's work. The kilns needed constant attention and the men slept in crude stone shelters between shifts, returning home late the following Friday. Sometimes they brought meat with them, which had been boiled at home, and added vegetables each day to make a broth, or *cawl*, heated on embers taken from the kilns. Accidents were commonplace and newspapers regularly reported deaths in the quarries. Quarrymen from Cornwall and Devon learned a crude form of Welsh, '*Cymraeg cerryg calch*' (limestone Welsh), to communicate with the other men.

Some farmers still burnt their own lime but most went to the quarries and bought what they needed. In 1882 David Davies hitched a horse and wagon and set off from Glanclawdd Farm, Gwynfe, where he worked for his uncle, to collect a load of lime. It was early in the morning and the sun had not yet reached the valley as he crossed the stream at Cwm Llwyd. It was going to be a long day for the young man. It was a steep climb along the small track leading up the mountain and it was some time before he reached the top. Loading the cart was heavy work and it was past eleven o'clock before he was ready to leave.

Davies' next journey was an eight-mile trek to the railway station at Llangadog, where he unloaded the lime and refilled the empty cart with coal. After a refreshing glass of beer at the Three Horseshoes he coaxed the tired horse back up the Black Mountain to the kilns, unloaded the coal and received payment for his day's work – a load of lime to spread on the fields of Glanclawdd Farm.

Davies was not looking forward to the journey home. The horse would have to strain every sinew to hold back the heavy wagon when they came down the mountain. As he climbed onto the wagon, something spooked the horse and it bolted. Davies fell beneath the wheels of the fully-loaded cart and was crushed. He died of his injuries, aged twenty-two.

The death of a young farm labourer made little difference to the industry and lime quarrying continued to expand until, in the twentieth century the quarries on the Black Mountain started to decline. The invention of Portland cement, manufactured in bulk, reduced demand for lime and prices fell. In an effort to stimulate agricultural output and help the struggling quarries, the government introduced a lime subsidy in 1937. By 1951 the subsidy amounted to 50 per cent of the cost of agricultural lime. The subsidy helped but many independent lime producers faced ruin, and Herbert's Quarry, the biggest on the mountain, went into receivership in 1952. In 1954 the owners of the land, Cawdor Estates, leased the quarry to Mr Richards and his partner Mr Llewellyn who restarted production. During the 1950s the lime subsidy was increased. Users were able to reclaim 60 per cent of the cost of agricultural lime.

According to claims made by the new operators, the quarry was soon producing record levels of lime, resulting in large subsidy payments. In 1959, the government increased the top rate of subsidy again, to 70 per cent and budgeted £10m per annum to fund the scheme. Producing agricultural lime had become a licence to print money, and once-worthless lime kilns were now valuable assets. Seeing an opportunity, the operators tried to sell Herbert's Quarry to Midas Quarries Limited. A price of more than £½ m was agreed plus an extra £24,000 for two lime kilns. A deposit of £82,000 was paid to seal the deal. When Midas Quarries examined the books they found that the lessees had exaggerated the output to increase the value of the quarry. Inspection of the quarry revealed that the kilns were faulty. One had not been fired for over ten years, and the crushing plant, needed to charge the kilns, was of little use. The only item in the quarry with any value was the weighbridge. The purchasers then discovered that the vendors of the quarry were lessees and the freehold belonged to Cawdor Estates. Midas Quarries were being swindled.

The fraud squad investigated and a major fraud was revealed. The quarry operators had been claiming money for lime that had not been manufactured. A paper trail of forged delivery notes and invoices led to more than 400 farmers being interviewed. Most were given immunity from prosecution in return for their cooperation. Agricultural wholesalers were implicated in the fraud. According to one report, if the output of the quarry claimed by the operators had been produced, Carmarthenshire would have been blanketed in 6 inches (150 mm) of lime. The case came to trial during the 1962 Winter Assizes in Carmarthen. Sir Alan Mocatta, an expert on restrictive practices, was the presiding judge. Sir Alan had previously been the Chairman of the Treasury Committee on Cheque Endorsement. The trial lasted fifty-five days and was, at the time, the longest criminal case in British history. It ended with the fraudsters being convicted and sent to prison.

Following the court case the quarry remained closed and there was a parliamentary enquiry into the abuse of lime subsidies.

Today the Black Mountain is owned by Brecon Beacon National Park Authority and nature is reclaiming the old workings. The weigh office and kilns can still be seen and an organisation called 'Calch' is making efforts to repair and preserve the heritage of the site. The lime subsidy was eventually withdrawn in 1976, after forty years of operation. Davies family members still live and farm near the Black Mountain and upland farmers still need to add lime to their land to maintain fertility. The stone commemorating David Davies vanished from the Black Mountain in the 1930s and was discovered fifty years later lying in a gutter. Two nieces of the dead man then approached Brecon Beacons National Park Authority who agreed to allow a new bilingual stone to be erected at the spot where the accident occurred. It was unveiled in December 1987 – 103 years after Davies died.

David Davies' memorial at the side of the road is small and the words on it only refer to one man's death but at the same time it reminds us of something bigger – a thriving industry that changed the shape of a mountain.

47

Penrice Folly Castle
Swansea

There are in fact two castles at Penrice, near Swansea (*Abertawe*). Following the Norman invasion in 1066, land on the Gower was given to one of William the Conqueror's knights in return for his services. The knight's family expanded its holdings and in about 1237 a descendant named Robert de Penres started to construct a castle at Penrice. The castle was positioned to take advantage of natural fortifications and was a formidable stronghold. It was further reinforced with extra curtain walls and flanking towers following a Welsh revolt in 1250. The Penres family continued to live at Penrice until the fourteenth century, when the male line died out and Penrice passed by marriage to the Mansel family. When the dissolution of the monasteries began, in 1536, Sir Rice Mansel shrewdly acquired 50,000 acres of land and the buildings which had belonged to Margam Abbey. At a stroke, the Mansels became landlords to most of the people living in Glamorgan.

When the 4th Baron Mansel died, the estates passed to the Reverend Thomas Talbot and then, in 1768, to his son Thomas Mansel Talbot. Thomas, who had just come of age, moved from Margam, took up residence at Penrice and built himself a new mansion below the castle. Thomas had recently returned from

Penrice Castle converted into a holiday cottage,
the style is more 'Disney' than Gothic

the Grand Tour, and during his time in Italy developed a taste for classical architecture and fine furnishings. Paying for the new house was not a problem for its new owner. An 1873 return declared that Margam Estate included 34,033 acres of land producing an annual rent of £44,175 (£4.1m in today's values). Other enterprises, including the docks at Port Talbot, were also producing substantial revenues.

The neo-classical mansion, confusingly also called Penrice Castle, was designed by the architect Anthony Keck who, it is believed, also designed Highgrove House in Gloucestershire, Prince Charles' residence. Thomas Mansel Talbot commissioned the landscape designer William Emes to design a park and when it was finished he described Penrice as 'the most romantic spot in all the county'.

It seems the twelfth-century castle, situated behind the mansion house, was not sufficiently romantic for the new owner so, in the 1790s, he built a mock castle ruin to form a new gatehouse. The mansion was enlarged twice during the nineteenth century, but in the 1830s the Talbot family moved out. Gothic architecture had become fashionable, and they took up residence in a new Gothic house in Margam, leaving Penrice empty except for the occasional visit.

During the early part of the twentieth century death duties caused the break-up of many country estates. The new tax, introduced in 1894, hit wealthy landowners hard, and land or other assets frequently had to be sold to raise the large sums of money demanded by the taxman when the owner died. Deaths which occurred close together could be devastating. Penrice continued to deteriorate until, in 1958, a new generation took over and began the painstaking work of restoring the house and parkland. The later Georgian and Victorian additions to the Mansion were demolished, new trees planted, and the park returned to its former beauty.

Today, Penrice Castle Estate is run as a tourism business, containing several holiday homes, and is available for hire as a film and television location. The folly castle, built by Thomas Mansel Talbot, has been skilfully converted into an eccentric-looking holiday cottage and is a Grade II* listed building.

48

Prospect Tower
Swansea

Robert Morris moved from Shropshire to Swansea, in 1724, to work as the manager of Llangyfelach Copper Works. When the proprietor of the factory was made bankrupt two years later, Morris took over the works and expanded it. An abundance of coal to fuel the factories and a safe harbour made Swansea a boom town. The industrial revolution was driving demand and people flocked to Swansea to find work in the new factories. Sheets of copper clad the bottom of ships. Copper pipes transported water, while copper alloys like brass and bronze were needed to make components for the new machinery that the factories required. The banks of the Tawe had become the most heavily industrialised place in the world, producing more than 60 per cent of the world's copper. Foul pollutants, indiscriminately discharged from the factories, killed everything in the river and the valley filled with acrid smog. 'Copperopolis' became the new name for the man-made hell on earth.

In 1768 Robert Morris died and his son, John, took over the business. John Morris was a shrewd businessman and diversified into coal mining. He was also a good employer, introducing innovative and previously unheard-of benefits for his workers. Morris created an injury compensation scheme, sick pay and

Prospect Tower, locked and boarded up to protect the bat colony that resides within

a pension plan. He built Morris Town for his workers, where each house had a garden large enough to grow vegetables for the family. Workers leased the plots for three lives (fifty years) at an annual rent of 7s 6d (37p). His more important labourers were allocated a plot of common land sufficient to keep a cow. Morris Town was completed in 1796 when it included 141 houses with 619 inhabitants. Today Morris Town is Morriston (*Treforys*), a suburb of Swansea.

In 1775, John Morris built Clasemont, a Palladian-style mansion, for himself at Pengwern, near the site of the present-day DVLA offices. Admiral Nelson and Lady Hamilton dined there with the copper magnate during their 1802 tour of Wales. Unfortunately, foul smoke drifting up the valley often filled the house so, in 1805, Clasemont was dismantled and rebuilt at Sketty.

Morris was involved in other projects and was the driving force behind the construction of the Swansea canal which was needed to transport coal from the upper valley. Its profitability can be gauged by the share price: shares issued for £11 in 1794 were worth £250 by 1834. Pentre Pit, one of Morris' coal mines, was continually flooding so, in 1778, he purchased a state of the art steam-driven pump from the Birmingham manufacturers Boulton and Watt. When it was installed it was the largest pump in the world, removing 1,000 gallons of water with each stroke – a staggering 72,000 gallons per hour.

John Morris became 1st Baronet of Clasemont in 1806 and died on 25 June 1819. During the 1820s his son, the 2nd Baronet, landscaped Sketty and built 'Prospect Tower,' a Gothic folly with fine views across the countryside.

Copper production in Swansea reached a peak in the 1880s with about 3-000 men working in the industry. By then, copper ore was being imported from as far away as Australia, South Africa and South America. Faced with the cost of importing ore, Swansea's producers became increasingly uncompetitive and the industry went into decline.

Swansea Corporation purchased Sketty Park in the 1930s and Clasemont was demolished, in 1975, so that a new housing estate could be built. In 2009 the boarded up Prospect Tower was put up for sale by the council as a potential 'grand design' project. A subsequent survey revealed that the derelict tower is the home of a rare species of bat and, as a result, no development would be allowed. The greater and lesser horseshoe bats inhabiting the folly have special legal protection and the tower was withdrawn from the market.

In 2014, Prospect Tower, once a proud building, stands squashed between modern houses on Saunders Way, Sketty, waiting for council bureaucrats to make a decision about its future.

49

Jersey Marine Tower
Swansea

In 1886, the brewer Captain Evan Evans was looking to diversify his business. Brewing beer was profitable but he wanted to expand and came up with an idea that would capitalise on a new industry – tourism. The growth of railways made it practical for ordinary people to travel, and the introduction of holidays gave them the opportunity.

The Bank Holidays Act of 1871 gave working people the legal right to four days' paid time off work, but it was not until 1936 that the Annual Holiday Bill legislated for the statutory right to a paid yearly holiday. The comfortably-off already visited spa towns like Bath and Harrogate, while the very rich enjoyed continental tours. The workers had few places they could afford to visit. Despite the delay in legislation, factory owners had already recognised the benefit of giving their employees paid holidays and, with money to spend, the workers wanted to enjoy themselves, forgetting their grim working conditions for a few days. New resorts like Llandudno were being developed to cater for the growing demand, and Captain Evans decided to invest in the new market.

The captain's plan was to build a holiday resort at Jersey Marine, an area of beaches and sand dunes between the river Neath and Swansea. The centre of

Jersey Marine Tower has been rescued and is now the centrepiece of an hotel

the complex was a four-storey octagonal tower with a 'camera obscura' at the top. Visitors would climb the tower and marvel at the view of Swansea and the surrounding landscape produced by the camera. It wasn't a new idea; camera obscuras – pin-hole cameras – had been around when the Greek Aristotle was alive. Competing resorts were busy building huge camera obscuras, and in 1896 the largest in the world was installed, on Constitution Hill at Aberystwyth, a record it still holds today.

Jersey Marine was a failure. The tower was built but, because of financial difficulties, the resort was not finished. According to local legend, the captain was at the top of the tower with a potential investor when he spied his daughter in the sand dunes and was mortified to see her cavorting with a young man. Having witnessed such a distressing scene, Captain Evans decided that he did not want visitors to be able to view such lewd behaviour through the camera obscura and it was never installed. The tower was boarded up and with the idea of building a tourist resort abandoned, Evans returned to his brewing business.

During the Second World War, the tower was a US Army observation post and American servicemen lived in the lower floors including, it is believed, a young man named Rocco Marchegiano. Rocco was a boxer who in 1946 won the American Amateur Armed Forces Championship. In 1948, he turned professional, changed his name to Rocky Marciano and became the Heavyweight Champion of the World. Marciano is the only heavyweight champion to remain undefeated throughout his career. Marciano's punch was tested in 1963 when *Boxing Illustrated* reported: 'Marciano's knockout blow packs more explosive energy than an armour-piercing bullet and represents as much energy as would be required to spot-lift 1000 pounds one foot off the ground.'

By the 1990s Jersey Marine Tower had no windows, ceiling or floors and was threatened with demolition. The building was saved when it was purchased and redeveloped as part of a new hotel complex. Jersey Marine Tower Hotel and Spa opened in 2006 and the centrepiece of the new hotel was the tower and its luxury top floor bridal suite. One hundred years after his original idea, a use had finally been found for Evans' Jersey Marine Tower in the growing hospitality industry.

Evan Evans brewery still brew excellent beer at Llandeilo and, in 2013, competed with 985 other breweries to win the coveted gold medal for the best organic bitter in the world. Described as the Oscars of the brewing world, it was a fitting accolade for a company created by a businessman bold enough to try new ideas, but with the courage to admit failure and give up.

50

Gnoll Belvedere
Neath

Sir Humphrey Mackworth was an industrialist, lawyer and fraudster who studied the scriptures in his spare time. He was educated at Oxford, graduating in 1674, and was knighted by Charles II in 1683 for his services to the legal profession. In 1686, Mackworth moved to Wales and married the heiress Mary Evans, still a minor, whose family owned the mineral rights in the Neath (*Nedd*) area. She died in 1696 and Mackworth inherited the Gnoll family estate. His diary revealed that he had always regarded the marriage and subsequent inheritance as a purely financial arrangement.

Although he now owned the Neath estate, the family had appointed David Evans to manage it. Mackworth, who believed in conspiracies wrote, 'Evans was resolved to ruin me.' Shortly afterwards the unfortunate manager suddenly died. Now in full control, Mackworth increased coal production and began to smelt copper. His next step was to acquire a large lead and silver mine in Cardiganshire but to do so he needed to raise more money. Mackworth took an office in Lincoln's Inn, London, and circulated prospectuses for a new company. The offer included exaggerated claims and a complicated lottery that would, supposedly, increase the returns to investors.

Gnoll Belvedere, a once grand building reduced to a ruin

With the share offer wildly oversubscribed, his Mine Adventurers' Company opened for business. Mackworth filled the board of directors with cronies and was free to do as he pleased. He used some of the monies received for charitable Christian purposes, a fact he would often refer to. The other share capital was invested in various dubious schemes.

In June 1699, Mackworth sent presents of coal to potential influential backers in an attempt to gain a parliamentary seat and followed up with lengthy letters asking for support in return for his future 'usefulness'.

Mackworth's direct strategy worked and he entered parliament in 1701. Shortly after gaining his seat he backed a bill aimed at preventing bribery during elections, an odd thing to do considering he had just bribed his way into the job. Mackworth was a pugnacious and active member of parliament, responsible for introducing a national system of workhouses. His continual intriguing and bullying made the new MP unpopular and he soon made enemies. In Wales, he was embroiled in a commercial war with his neighbour Sir Edward Mansel. The Mansel mines at Briton Ferry competed directly with Mackworth's and the rivalry was personal. To make matters worse in Mackworth's mine, coal output slowed because of a mutiny by the men, and mobs from Neath, upset by his spiteful behaviour, attacked his coal wagons.

Mackworth responded through the courts but ran up against the influence of his powerful neighbours. In 1708, he lost his seat and the legal protection it afforded. The creditors and investors of the Mine Adventurers' Company petitioned parliament, alleging mismanagement and fraud. The petition was received and a committee reported without bothering to hear Mackworth's defence. Mackworth attempted to blame his agent William Waller who responded by publishing letters from Mackworth. The correspondence showed Humphrey Mackworth to be ruthless, devious, hypocritical, self-seeking and corrupt. His reputation was in ruins.

Sourly, Waller wrote:

a gentleman who at the beginning of the undertaking owed for his new chambers in

Lincoln's Inn and owned that he had not paid for an estate he bought in Cardiff ... but by his wonderful management of affairs since, has bought no less than nine lordships in the same county and has found money, either of his own, or somebody else's, to pay for them all.

Parliament found Mackworth 'guilty of many notorious frauds, and indirect practices in violation of the charter granted to the said company, in breach of trust and to the manifest wrong and oppression of the proprietors and creditors'.

Surprisingly, Mackworth survived, was re-elected to Parliament and began a long fight to regain control of his company. 1720 was a boom year and the directors of the Mine Adventurer's Company wanted to raise capital in order to expand. When they made a share issue, Mackworth borrowed heavily and bought as many shares as possible. Then, he forced a general meeting, packed it with supporters and got himself elected governor. He was back in charge once more.

Sir Humphrey Mackworth spent the last ten years of his life engaging in litigation with the conspirators he felt surrounded by. He died of fever on 25 August 1727 at Gnoll. At the time his assets amounted to £14,450 and he owed more than £17,000. The cunning old rogue was penniless.

Following Sir Humphrey's death, Gnoll passed to his son, Herbert Mackworth, a Lieutenant Colonel of the Glamorgan militia and Fellow of the Royal Society, described as 'a gentleman well versed in natural history and every branch of mathematics and philosophical thinking'. He was made a baronet in 1776.

Herbert Mackworth was a keen horticulturalist and employed twenty-eight gardeners at Gnoll. He enlarged the house and made architectural improvements to the garden, including adding ponds, a water cascade and the 'Belvedere.' Belvedere is an Italian word meaning 'beautiful sight,' and refers to the banqueting tower he built on a hill above the house. After the Belvedere was constructed it became covered with ivy, and was known as the Ivy Tower – a name still used on Ordnance Survey maps. The Belvedere contained a dining room on the first floor and caretaker's flat in the basement. Herbert enjoyed treating his guests to a tour of the gardens followed by afternoon tea in the Belvedere.

In 1791, while gardening, a thorn stuck in Herbert Mackworth's finger. He did not seek medical attention immediately for such a minor wound, but died a month later of blood poisoning.

Within a year, the next Mackworth, Robert married a 16-year-old girl named Mary Ann. Robert died two years later, leaving Mary, or Molly as she was known, a widow alone at Gnoll.

Mary Ann sold up in 1811, remarried and moved out. During the next century, Gnoll House had a variety of occupiers until 1923 when Neath Borough Council bought it. The last gamekeeper of the estate had lived in the Belvedere until 1920, when it was gutted by fire. The council had no practical use for the house and it continued to deteriorate. It was demolished in 1957.

In 1984, restoration work began on the gardens which have since become a country park. Although there is little left of the structure except some of the outer walls the Belvedere remains one of the most prominent features in the area. The building is listed but, like Sir Humphrey Mackworth's reputation, it is unlikely to be saved.

51

Dunraven Garden Tower
Bridgend

Dunraven (*Dyndryfan*), which some believe means 'three-sided fortress' (although it's not a true translation), was once an Iron Age Hillfort occupied by the Silures, an ancient British tribe. Their chief, Caradog (known to the Romans as Caractacus), led an effective ten-year campaign against invading Romans, who responded by establishing a large garrison at Caerleon. Silure lookouts at Dyndryfan watched Roman vessels bringing reinforcements up the Bristol Channel to Caerleon. In about AD 50, Caradog was overwhelmed and his army beaten in battle. Caradog escaped north but was betrayed by another tribe and handed to the Romans in irons. Despite losing their leader, the Silures fought on for another thirty years.

Caradog was taken to Rome and paraded before Emperor Claudius, expecting to be strangled, the normal fate of captured enemy leaders. Brought before the emperor, Caradog made a passionate speech explaining why his peoples fought against the tyranny of Roman rule. Claudius was so impressed by the eloquence with which Caradog defended his actions that he reprieved the Silurian king and allowed him to live out his days in Rome as a free man.

During the eleventh century, the Normans

Dunraven Ice House, the door leading to the buried chamber is hidden at the back

occupied Glamorgan and built a castle at nearby Ogmore. The new lord, Maurice de Londres, visited Cydweli and left his steward, Arnold de Boteler, in charge, whereupon the Welsh attacked. De Boteler successfully defended the castle and was given the Manor of Dyndryfan as a reward for his actions. The names of Boteler and his estate became anglicized over the years to Butler and Dunraven. The last Butler, another Arnold, died in 1541, and the estate became the property of Walter Vaughn of Hereford, the most notorious owner of Dunraven.

According to legend, Walter Vaughn was a ship-wrecker, who added to his fortune by using lamps to lure ships onto the rocks below the cliffs, where they ran aground and were looted. When two of his sons who were out fishing were caught up in a sudden squall, Vaughn watched helplessly as their boat foundered and the boys drowned. His third son had earlier left home to start a new life. Later, while wrecking another vessel onto the rocks, Vaughn watched with contempt as the sailors tried to save themselves by swimming ashore. Only one man reached the beach and, because he was a potential witness, the robbers killed him and stole a ring from his dead finger. When Vaughn saw the ring he realised, to his horror, that the murdered sailor was his last remaining son, returning home. Because of his evil deeds the headland where he plied the evil trade became known as 'Witches Point'.

According to the story, Vaughn went mad, and a short while later Dunraven was sold.

In 1642, Dunraven was bought by the Sir Humphrey Wyndham, a Norfolk gentleman with Saxon roots. The Wyndhams added a deer park to the estate and built kennels for his foxhounds. These are now used as a Heritage Visitor Centre. Until 1803, Dunraven House was a modest dwelling, but that changed when Mrs Thomas Wyndham decided to rebuild it. She drafted her own architectural designs and her husband oversaw the building work, creating Dunraven Castle, a mock castle complete with battlements.

In 1824, Caroline Wyndham-Quin and her husband, who was by then 2nd Earl Dunraven, inherited. Caroline was a great benefactor. She paid for a church and a school to be built at Clearwell and for the first mains water supply to be installed in Bridgend (*Pen-y-bont ar Ogwr*). Caroline's hobby was horticulture. She added a spectacularly large conservatory to the castle, extended the walled gardens and built a medieval style tower on an earth mound.

Another notable family member was the 4th Earl, Thomas Wyndham-Quin KP, PC, CMG, OBE, Lieutenant of County Limerick, JP of Glamorgan, Hon. Colonel of the 5th Battalion, Royal Munster Fusiliers, the 23rd Armoured Car Company and the TA. The Earl was a keen yachtsman and owned a fabulous racing yacht which he sailed in races against the Prince of Wales. The 4th Earl died in 1926.

During the First and Second World Wars Dunraven Castle was requisitioned and used as a military hospital, during which time it deteriorated. After the wars, a caretaker remained in residence but the family never returned to live there. Dunraven was used briefly as a holiday hostel during the 1950s, but in 1962 the contents were auctioned. The house was demolished in 1963 leaving some foundations, the walled garden and the curious medieval turret standing at its corner.

At first sight, the tower appears to be a folly, but it contains a secret. At the base of the tower, which, as mentioned above, is on a mound, there is a small door. The door leads to a narrow 20-feet (6 metres) long passageway and three airlocks, beyond which there is a circular chamber 13 feet (4 metres) deep. The roof of the chamber is vaulted and its walls are more than 5 feet (2.5 metres) thick. It was for use as an ice house. Ice packed into the subterranean chamber during the winter months kept Dunraven Castle supplied through the year.

The folly tower was renovated in the 1980s. Restoration work continues on the walled gardens and today the gardens, headland and beach are open to the public, courtesy of the Trustees of Dunraven Estate and the Countryside Commission. The spectacular coastline of 200-feet high cliffs and sea-level limestone pavements, often used as a location for television and film productions including the BBC series *Doctor Who*, make the Dunraven site well worth a visit.

52

Roath Park Clock Tower
Cardiff

In 1909, a young naval lieutenant named Edward Evans met with the editor of the *Western Mail* in Cardiff (*Caerdydd*). The lieutenant was canvassing for support to mount an expedition to Antarctica. Evans, an experienced navigator who had been on previous expeditions, was persuasive, and the editor, William Davies, quickly agreed to help promote the planned project. He saw it as a Welsh adventure and his paper would be instrumental in raising the profile of the endeavour by asking the public to give generously to pay for the equipment needed.

While Evans was busy raising funds, other adventurers were planning similar expeditions. Roald Amundsen, a Norwegian explorer, was assembling his own team, intent on reaching the South Pole first. A third contender, Robert Falcon Scott, was also preparing to be the first human to travel to the most southerly point on the planet. Scott was a polar explorer who had commanded previous expeditions and had experience of sledging long distances across the frozen ice.

At the same time, another British explorer was also attempting to reach the South Pole. Ernest Shackleton's expedition of 1909 failed, and was forced to turn back less than 100 miles from the pole. The

Roath Park Clock Tower, erected in 1915 to honour Captain Scott's doomed expedition to the South Pole

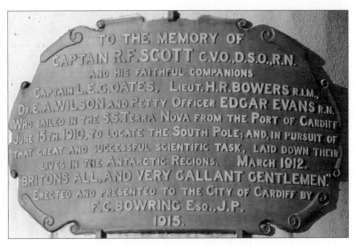

TO THE MEMORY OF
CAPTAIN R.F.SCOTT C.V.O.,D.S.O.,R.N.
AND HIS FAITHFUL COMPANIONS
CAPTAIN L.E.G.OATES, LIEUT. H.R.BOWERS R.I.M.,
DR.E.A.WILSON AND PETTY OFFICER EDGAR EVANS R.N.
WHO SAILED IN THE S.S.TERRA NOVA FROM THE PORT OF CARDIFF
JUNE 15TH 1910, TO LOCATE THE SOUTH POLE; AND, IN PURSUIT OF
THAT GREAT AND SUCCESSFUL SCIENTIFIC TASK, LAID DOWN THEIR
LIVES IN THE ANTARCTIC REGIONS.   MARCH 1912.
"BRITONS ALL, AND VERY GALLANT GENTLEMEN."
ERECTED AND PRESENTED TO THE CITY OF CARDIFF BY
F.C.BOWRING ESQ.,J.P.
1915.

The plaque on the clock tower

British expedition that Shackleton led almost ended in tragedy. Facing a foreign challenge from Amundsen, Evans and Scott agreed to pool their resources and take a joint expedition. Scott would lead and Evans would be second in command. Scott is quoted as saying, 'The main objective of this expedition is to reach the South Pole and to secure for the British Empire the honour of this achievement'.

By then, the *Western Mail*'s fund-raising campaign was in full swing. £40,000 would have to be raised for the expedition to go ahead. £2,500 was collected on the streets of Cardiff. The Welsh Tinplate Company donated cooking utensils. School children gave their pocket money to pay for sleeping bags. Coal was needed to fire the ship's boilers and the best available was Welsh Steam Coal, which burned hotter and longer, making less ash. Coal companies offered 100 tons of coal, together with 300 gallons of petrol, lamp oil and 500 gallons of diesel. The Welsh politician David Lloyd George, Chancellor of the Exchequer, provided a government grant of £20,000. Commercial sponsors such as the 'OXO' food company were invited to help, and eventually the target was reached.

The *SS Terra Nova* was obtained for £12,500. Despite her poor condition, the vessel proved to be the most expensive single purchase. The *Terra Nova* had sailed to the Antarctic on previous expeditions but it was unlikely that the Board of Trade would allow her to sail; she did not comply with the current safety standards. To circumvent Board of Trade regulations, Scott paid £100 to become a member of the Royal Yacht Squadron. This exempted him from Board of Trade rules, enabling him to sail under a White Ensign flag, and command the ship according to naval regulations.

The *Terra Nova* was moved to Bute Dock in Cardiff where she was fuelled and provisioned, thanks to the generosity of Cardiff ship-owners and the people of Wales. In recognition of the help Wales had given to the coming adventure, Cardiff was registered as the *Terra Nova*'s home port. She sailed for the Antarctic on 15 June 1910. On board were sixty-five officers and men. Scott was not among them. He joined the ship later when it reached South Africa. When the *Terra Nova* arrived in Melbourne, Scott received a telegram from Amundsen saying that Amundsen was proceeding south. It was to be a race to the South Pole.

Before reaching Antarctica the *Terra Nova* experienced violent storms. The bilge pumps failed and the crew resorted to bailing water using buckets. The ship arrived in January 1911 and the explorers set up camp, building prefabricated huts and using ponies to drag supplies ashore. The next four months were spent establishing supply depots further south. On 23 April the sun set for the winter and the men retreated to their accommodation. Perpetual darkness and extreme cold made working outside impossible for five tedious months. Scott maintained strict discipline during the dark winter months, with officers and men separated by a partition of packing cases.

The weather began to improve and, on 13 September, the 800-mile trek to the South Pole began. Sixteen men made up the party using motor sledges augmented with ponies and dogs. The animals were to prove more reliable than the machines. The plan was to send groups back at various points after supplies were cached for use on the return journey. As the sledges emptied, ponies with nothing to drag were shot for food. The original plan was for four men to make it to the South Pole but Scott increased the team to five, causing problems with provisions. Food and fuel for cooking had only been prepared for a four-man party.

The five men chosen for the final leg of the journey were Scott himself, Captain Oates, Wilson, Bowers and Edgar Evans (not to be confused with Edward Evans.) They reached the pole on 17 January 1912. To their dismay a black flag, left by Amundsen, was already there. The Norwegian had beaten Scott's party by thirty-four days. After resting and posing for some pictures they began the long trek back. On 4 February Edgar Evans, who had become unwell, suffered a fall and died. The remaining four men still had hundreds of miles to walk. Eventually, after many days of clambering across the ice, the exhausted, hungry men pitched their tent and retreated inside. An old war wound had flared up, making it difficult for Oates to walk. He knew that he was slowing the others down. Scott's diary records Captain Oates' last words: I am just going outside and may be some time'. He left the tent and was never seen again.

Scott, Wilson and Bowers trudged a further 20 miles but they never reached safety. The frozen bodies of Scott and his two companions were discovered by a search party on 12 November. Oates' body was never found. Scott and his party had walked more than 1,500 miles before dying from a combination of starvation and scurvy. They were within 11 miles of the next supply depot.

Earlier, Edward Evans, Scott's second-in-command, had been setting up supply depots when he also contracted scurvy and nearly died. At the time, the importance of a diet containing Vitamin C to combat scurvy was not appreciated. Because of his illness, the Welshman was repatriated on the *Terra Nova* in March 1912. He recovered from the disease and commanded the *Terra Nova* when it returned to Antarctica the following year to rescue the expedition's survivors. Evans continued his naval career, saw action in the First World War and retired as an admiral, having been made a baronet. He also formalised the rule for professional wrestling, known today as 'Admiral Lord Mountevans Rules'. Previously, 'all-in' wrestling, which the rules replaced, had become a very violent sport.

Scott's Antarctic expedition has been the subject of much debate. Some claimed that Scott was a reckless adventurer who risked the lives of his men. Others, that he was a meticulous leader whose orders were disobeyed, costing him his life. According to reports, he left written instructions for a support party to head south, towards the men returning from the pole, but they didn't go. Had the relief party set out, as instructed, Scott and his companions might have been rescued. Was Scott's decision to increase the size of the polar party from four to five the reason they never got back? We shall never know. One fact is certain. It was the support of the people of Wales, and Cardiff in particular, that made the expedition possible. Without their generosity, it is doubtful if Scott and his expedition would have reached the South Pole and there would be no legendary 'Scott of the Antarctic'.

In 1914, a boating lake in Roath Park, Cardiff was drained so that foundations could be laid for a peculiar building. The tower, in the shape of a lighthouse, contains a clock and above it is a model of the *SS Terra Nova*. The Clocktower, Lighthouse, Scott Memorial – it goes by a variety of names – was unveiled in 1915, having cost £159 6s 8d to build. It's a pretty object and an appropriate cenotaph for such brave men.

53

Dr Price's Roundhouses
Pontypridd

William Price was born on 4 March 1800. His father was an educated priest who had been to Jesus College, Oxford, and his mother was an uneducated Welsh servant girl. Following his birth William's father suffered from a mental illness involving eccentric behaviour and bouts of violence. The illiterate William did not begin his schooling until the age of ten. He was a quick learner and caught up rapidly. Within three years he was apprenticed to a doctor and by 1821 he was a qualified surgeon working in London.

Dr Price returned to Wales with radical ideas planning to establish his own practice in Pontypridd. Price encouraged his patients to exercise, eat a healthy vegetarian diet and refused to treat smokers, ideas that, 150 years later, have been recognised as common sense. The doctor refused to wear socks, saying they were unhygienic, and he washed any money he was paid before reusing it. He operated a flexible pricing policy, charging what he considered his patients could afford. In some cases, Dr Price treated patients for free. The people of Pontypridd soon accepted their strange new doctor and his practice flourished.

As well as having revolutionary ideas about health and medical services, the doctor was a Welsh Nationalist and a practising druid, both of which

Dr Price's Round Houses,
all that remains of his planned museum and free school

would become more extreme as he grew older. Seeing the plight of the poor, Price became a Chartist, vigorously supporting emancipation for the working classes. He could see no excuse for denying a man the vote because he did not own property. Conflict with his wealthier clients, caused by his Chartism, strengthened his opinions and made the doctor even more ardent in his beliefs. Wanting to take direct action to help the poor, he established Pontypridd Provision Company. It was the first Co-operative Society in Wales.

In 1839, following a failed Chartist uprising in which he was involved, Price fled to France where he remained for two years.

During his time in France, Dr Price's attitudes

hardened and he convinced himself that he would return to Wales and liberate the people from English domination. Price spent his time studying the ancient Celtic religion and claimed to have translated druid inscriptions he found on Greek monuments in Paris museums. When he returned to Wales, Price had grown his hair long and stopped shaving.

As the doctor's ideas became more extreme, so too did his style of dress. He dressed in an emerald coat with a scarlet sash and wore a fox-head fur cap. Price announced that he was a druid priest who would revive druidic practices, and walked with a staff engraved with druid writing. He declared that marriage was an abomination that enslaved women. During most of his life the doctor practised free love, fathering children by at least two women. His bizarre attire and strange attitudes led to confrontations with the authorities, and Price was a frequent visitor to the law courts. On one occasion he fought a case to have his father exhumed to test for insanity. On another he was accused of the manslaughter of a patient. Price always conducted his own cases, was a capable orator and pugnacious opponent. He usually won.

To spread druidism, Dr Price held an eisteddfod in Pontypridd in 1844. Unfortunately, no one turned up. Undeterred, Price continued with the event and initiated his daughter as a bard. Next, Doctor Price turned his attention to building a druid museum and free school for the poor. He approached the politician, Sir Benjamin Hall, 1st Baron Llanover (after whom the parliamentary bell 'Big Ben' is reputedly named) for help. Sir Benjamin and his wife supported Welsh culture and, unusually for the time, encouraged the use of the Welsh language on their estates. Sir Benjamin agreed to back the project and allowed Dr Price the use of some of his land in Pontypridd.

Price engaged builders and work began on a magnificent gatehouse, comprising two roundhouses that would serve as the entrance to the museum and school. Unfortunately, Lady Llanover fell out with Dr Price and in 1861, with the gatehouse nearing completion, the project was abruptly cancelled. The reason for her dislike is unclear, but it has been suggested by others that Lady Llanover was upset when Price made an inappropriate advance towards her. Discovering that the doctor did not own the land they had built on, the builders pursued him for their money. Unable to pay the debt, he fled back to France.

Price returned to Wales in 1866 and set up as a doctor in Llantrisant, engaging Gwenllian Llywelyn, a young farmer's daughter, as his housekeeper. Despite his distaste for marriage Dr Price married Gwenllian in a druidic ceremony in 1881. The 81-year-old doctor's new wife was thirty-six. Their first child, named *Iesu Grist* (Jesus Christ), was born in 1883 and died five months later. According to his druidic beliefs, Dr Price carried the body to Caerlan Hill and cremated it using a tray of paraffin and some rags. Onlookers were horrified and he was arrested for the illegal disposal of a corpse.

During the court case, Price defended himself and argued 'That while the law did not state that cremation was legal, it also did not state that it was illegal'. He won the argument and was released by the presiding judge. It was a sensational case attracting nationwide publicity and made the eccentric doctor famous. The precedent he established led to the creation of the Cremation Society of Great Britain and the Cremation Act of 1904.

Dr Price's statue showing him in his strange druid regalia

On 23 January 1893, aged ninety-three, Dr Price slipped and fell off a chair. He called for Gwenllian to bring some champagne, sipped a glass and died. According to his written instructions, his body was carried to the place where he had cremated his son. The corpse was laid on a funeral pyre containing two tons of coal and the blaze was ignited. Tickets were sold for the event and a crowd of over 20,000 people stood on Caerlan Hill to watch the cremation.

Regarded by many as an eccentric crank and others as an enlightened radical man, Dr Price was certainly a revolutionary figure. Today, over 100 years later, many of his views are quite acceptable. The Pontypridd roundhouses never served as a gatehouses but they stand to remind us of Doctor William Price, member of the Royal College of Surgeons, Welsh patriot, druid and original thinker, a man the historian Ronald Hutton described as 'One of the most colourful characters in Welsh history and one of the most remarkable in Victorian Britain'.

54

Hy-Brasail House
Merthyr Tudful

To the north of Merthyr Tydful, near the railway viaduct at Pontsarn, stands a very peculiar house. The property has been known by a number of different names over the years, including Hafod Cottage, Vaynor Cottage, The Old Spanish House and, more recently, Hy Brasail. At the time of writing, the house, Grade II listed, stands empty, neglected and looking very sad. What makes the house unique is the style in which it was built.

Like its name, Hy Brasail, the house, is shrouded in mystery. Some commentators have suggested that the house was named after 'Hy Brasail' – also known as 'Hy Brasil' – a mythical island somewhere off the coast of Ireland. According to legend, the island is hidden by an inpenetrable mist except for one day every seven years. In the old Irish tongue the name of the island suggests beauty, great worth and might. In 1674, a Captain Nisbet was on a voyage from France to Ireland when he chanced upon the mysterious island. According to the Captain's reports, a colony of enormous black rabbits inhabited the island, together with a magician who lived alone in a castle. It's an unlikely tale and a strange place after which to name a house near Merthyr Tydful.

As well as having a strange name, the house called

Hy-Brasail house built, it is said,
to impress an Italian Countess

Hy Brasail is a bewilderment of ideas. Part of the dwelling is conventional and looks like a Victorian middle class house but a strange extension has been added. Stone columns hold up an incongruous arch while, just beyond, Spanish archways support an upper floor containing stone-mullioned windows, sheltering from the weather under a Welsh slate roof. Alongside the mullioned windows, an upstairs veranda sits, surrounded by carved stone balustrades. To add to the discord, two Venetian stone towers emerge, like campaniles, from the roof. Even the towers, with their pink stone columns, are mismatched; one is larger than the other.

There are several opinions regarding the origins of the strange dwelling. Although there is no evidence to support the idea, some say it was built by an owner in the style of his wife's Tuscan childhood home. It is known that a solicitor named Mr James, whose law practice was in Merthyr, lived in the house in 1912. At the time the house, rather smaller than it is now, was known as 'Vaynor Cottage.' Each morning, Mr James walked to Pontsarn Station to catch an early train to Merthyr. Each night he returned to his empty house. That summer, he went to Italy for a holiday met an Italian Contessa, and immediately fell in love.

Thinking the holiday liaison was something more serious than a brief romance, Mr James returned home and added an Italian-style extension to his house with the hope that the Contessa would join him in Wales. To make the house more homely, he furnished it with fine furniture, porcelain and paintings, and in the courtyard, at the front of the house, he placed a large statue of an eagle sitting on a plinth. Sadly, the Contessa never came to Wales and Mr James' dream of love remained unfulfilled. The disappointed solicitor resumed his daily train rides to work and remained a bachelor for the rest of his life.

In 1948, a butcher by the name of Bowen bought Vaynor Cottage. Bowen's Irish wife, a teacher, wanted a name for the house that was more in keeping with its size and quirky character. It was Mrs Bowen who renamed the house 'Hy Brasail' after the mythical island from Irish folklore.

The eagle was either sold or stolen in the 1980s, and the railway station at Pontsarn has long since closed. Today, the old rail bed is part of the Taff Trail, and walkers who enjoy the path pass close to Hy Brasail, a structurally odd derelict building and one of the strangest-looking houses in Wales.

55

Nantyglo Roundhouses
Merthyr Tudful

In the nineteenth century, the south Wales valleys underwent dramatic industrial change. People arrived in their thousands looking for work, and ruthless ironmasters made fortunes. Workers were expendable and open to mistreatment. Wages in the ironworks were minimal and depended on output. Men were paid with tokens that could only be used in company-owned shops. These 'Truck Shops', as they were known, sold goods with inflated prices to increase the ironmasters's profits even more. Overcrowded and insanitary housing, owned by the ironmasters, came with the job. To lose your job meant that your family became homeless. There were no unions to protect the men from exploitation and a surplus pool of immigrant labour made it possible for the ironmasters to drive wages down to subsistence levels. South Wales was booming, but it was a powder keg waiting to explode.

Joseph Bailey was a young man when he left his family home in Yorkshire and walked to Merthyr Tydfil to visit his rich uncle, Richard Crawshay. Crawshay, also a Yorkshire man, had made a vast fortune and was possibly the most famous of the ironmasters. The two men got on well and Crawshay took Joseph into the business. Crawshay died in 1810

The southern Nantyglo roundhouse was blown up in the 1940s

The northern roundhouse, still intact and a formidable bastion

*The musket firing slots in the door at knee height
can be clearly seen*

and left a quarter of his iron foundry to Bailey. Joseph
Bailey, who wanted to be his own boss, sold his share
for £20,000 and bought Nantyglo Ironworks.
Nantyglo means 'brook of coal' and the area was rich
in the natural resources needed to feed a foundry. The
works had been closed for some time but was soon
brought back into production. Iron production
slumped in the 1810s but, perhaps because of Bailey's
ruthless approach, Nantyglo prospered and was the
only foundry to increase its output. The foundry
supplied much of the railway track needed to traverse
North America, and went on to become one of the
most important ironworks in Britain. At its peak, the
foundry employed 3,500 workers, including 500
women.

As the business prospered, resentment and industrial unrest increased. Militant workers, known as 'Scotch Cattle', accused immigrant Irish workers of stealing jobs and threatened to kill them. The situation looked ugly. In 1816, Bailey attempted to reduce his men's wages again, resulting in a riot at the Nantyglo foundry. Eventually, the ironmaster withdrew the threatened wage reduction and things calmed down. It was a warning that Joseph Bailey did not ignore. In response, he built two roundhouses at Nantyglo. The roundhouses were fortified redoubts, designed as refuges; he and his family could retreat into the event of any insurrection. The Nantyglo Roundhouses would be the last private fortifications to be built in Britain.

The stone roundhouses had cellars, well stocked with provisions to withstand a siege. The outer walls were 4 feet thick and were reinforced with cast iron beams. Both towers had a cast iron roof, overlaid with bricks and pitch. The windows had cast iron frames and tapered outwards, making them easier to defend. The doors, also cast iron, incorporated firing slots from which muskets could be fired to deter attackers. Shutters covered the inside of the firing positions when not in use.

More civil unrest followed in 1822, when Joseph Bailey arbitrarily cut his men's wages. Troops were billeted near the roundhouses to intimidate the workers and deter them from reacting. Worse was to follow.

In 1831, the Merthyr Riots erupted, and brought

the tense situation to a violent climax. Armed workers took to the streets and before long much of south Wales was in open rebellion. The authorities reacted by ordering the army to put down the insurrection. Argyll and Sutherland Highlanders were shipped from Scotland to deal with the rioters. To begin with the soldiers were poorly prepared and were routed by the well-organised rioters. The inevitable showdown came when 450 troops, with fixed bayonets, broke up a mass rally at Dowlais; forty were killed (including sixteen soldiers), and many injured. This crushed the workers' resolve. The rebellion had effectively ended.

There was another, vindictive, final act to follow. Lord Melbourne, a leading political figure, insisted that at least one rioter should be executed as an example to the rest. Several men were tried as conspirators and Richard Lewis, a 23-year-old miner (also known as Dic Penderyn, after his home village), was charged with stabbing a soldier in the leg. He protested his innocence throughout the trial but was convicted and sentenced to death. A huge public outcry against the punishment produced an 11,000 signature petition pleading for his release. Despite this, he went to the scaffold still shouting that he was innocent of any crime. Years later, a witness who had helped convict Penderyn admitted that he had lied, on the instruction of Lord Melbourne, sending a blameless man to the gallows.

It's not clear if the roundhouses at Nantyglo were used as redoubts during the riots. Later, they served as houses and for storage until, in 1885, the contents were sold off. Joseph Bailey retired from business to live on his country estate at Glanusk, Crickhowell. Having passed the responsibility of running the foundry on to others, he went into politics, eventually becoming Lord Glanusk. He died in 1858. In 1869, the Bailey family disposed of their shares in Nantyglo Ironworks and the foundry eventually closed. It was dismantled in 1878.

In 1831, Parliament passed legislation known as the Truck Act outlawing the practice of paying workers in company tokens, but it was not until 1867 that a Royal Commission recommended that trade unions, which could protect working men's right, should be decriminalised. They were legalised four years later, in 1871.

In the 1940s, explosives were used to partially demolish the southern roundhouse so that scrap iron could be stripped from the ruin.

The northern roundhouse was restored in the 1980s. Today, it's a Grade II listed building and a potent reminder of a time when men lived in fear of their masters, and masters were afraid of their men.

56

The Folly Tower
Pontypool

On high ground between Pontypool and Monmouthshire stands a tower from where, on a clear day, it is claimed, seven counties can be seen. The octagonal tower, some 40 feet (12 metres) tall, has been repaired and rebuilt a number of times. An 1865 article in the *Monmouthshire Free Press* described it thus: 'an elevated spot where a Tower (formerly a Roman watch-tower) was many years since rebuilt as an observatory and which is popularly known as The Folly.' The newspaper was referring to a tower that had been built 100 years earlier, by a landowner named Major Hanbury.

John Hanbury was an ironmaster who made a fortune by developing a process to roll metal into thin sheets and coat it with tin to prevent rusting. As a result, Pontypool became an important centre for tinplate manufacturing. Hanbury used his money to acquire Pontypool House and commissioned the landscape designer Capability Brown to plan a park around the house.

By 1831 the tower was falling into disrepair and the major's son, now the owner of Pontypool House, had the folly renovated. In 1935 the tower was the focal point of a bonfire party, attended by more than 15,000 people, to celebrate the Silver Jubilee of King George

V. Shortly after the party, Pontypool House Estates Office put up notices, warning people to keep away and beware of falling masonry. Once again the tower was becoming unsafe.

The condition of the tower continued to deteriorate and by the outbreak of World War II in 1939, it was in a poor state. As well as being dangerous to passers-by, the War Office considered the tower to be a danger to a factory some miles to the east. It was believed that the Luftwaffe might use the tower as a navigation marker to identify the Royal Ordnance Factory at Glascoed. ROF Glascoed had recently been built to manufacture munitions and, with extensive underground magazines, was considered an important target for German bombers. In 1940, the War Office ordered the folly tower be demolished. During the war, Glascoed munitions factory was only bombed twice – probably by accident. The bombs killed just one of the 13,000 workers. Debriefed German aircrews, mistakenly, reported that they had bombed an airfield near Bristol. The location of

Folly Tower Pontypool, dismantled during World War II and rebuilt in 1994

ordnance factories was a closely guarded secret and since none were identified on any maps, it's quite possible that the German High Command did not know of ROF Glascoed's existence.

At the end of the war, Pontypool Chamber of Trade started a campaign to rebuild the tower. Public collections were arranged, but the scheme was blocked at a council meeting in 1948 when council members voted to spend any funds available on the rebuilding and repairing of bomb damaged housing. More than forty years would pass before another attempt was made to resurrect Folly Tower.

In 1990 a committee was established to try again and money from a variety of funds was applied for. £60,000 was raised and that October, Brecon Beacons National Park Authority gave planning permission to rebuild the tower. Work began in May 1991, using 175 metric tons of donated stone, recovered from a recently demolished school. The tower was officially reopened on July 22 1994. A plaque commemorating the occasion reads:

Folly Tower, Rebuilt 1994.
This scheme has been financed by the European Regional Development Fund, Torfaen Borough, Croft Pontypool, Gwent County Council, The Prince of Wales' Committee

There may have been a tower at this spot since Roman times, but the folly that stands in Pontypool Park today is only twenty years old.

57

The Shell Grotto
Pontypool

A 'grotto' (Italian '*grotta*' and French '*grotte*') is any type of natural or artificial cave associated with modern, historic or prehistoric human use. The Shell Grotto at Pontypool is regarded by some as the finest surviving grotto in Wales. Like its neighbour Folly Tower, the grotto was built by John Hanbury, the ironmaster and owner of Pontypool House. Built in the late 1800s, the grotto is on a ridge 700 feet (213 metres) above sea level, making it a prominent landmark with superb views in all directions.

Viewed from the outside, the grotto resembles an unusual cottage with curved stone walls and windows that appear to have been acquired from a church. Inside, the vaulted roof is supported on six pillars. This unusual shape, together with the fact that surfaces are covered with thousands of seashells, gives a surreal feeling to the grotto. Although John Hanbury is understood to have built the grotto it was his daughter-in-law, Molly Hanbury Leigh, who added the shell decorations during renovation work done much later. In the nineteenth century, using seashells to embellish grottos had become fashionable, and Molly was known to be an enthusiastic shell collector. The grotto was used for family picnics and also during shoots on the estate;

*Shell Grotto Pontypool where Edward the Prince of Wales
once enjoyed a picnic*

there are accounts that the Prince of Wales, later King
Edward VII, enjoyed a picnic there.

In the 1920, Pontypool House became a Roman
Catholic school and the parkland, including the
grotto, was purchased by the local authority. In the
years that followed, the grotto was neglected and its
condition deteriorated. Woodworm ate the timbers.
The roof collapsed and the walls crumbled. Vandals
also caused considerable damage to the interior. In
the 1990s, attitudes to conservation were changing as
the authorities began to realise the importance of
protecting historic buildings. Welsh Heritage, Cadw
and the European Regional Development Fund paid
for major renovation work to be undertaken on the
grotto. This was followed by extensive repairs to the

shell interior, using old photographs to ensure authenticity. The work was completed in 1996 and the grotto, which now stands within Pontypool Park, is open to the public at certain times of the year on weekends and bank holidays.

58

Clytha Castle
Abergavenny

The practice of erecting a memorial to a loved one is common enough, but when William Jones' wife Elizabeth died in 1787 he felt that something better than a tombstone was required. Marrying Elizabeth had made Jones a wealthy man. One cynical commentator of the period described her as 'the female heir of the House of Tredegar, who bestowed on the proprietor a splendid fortune'. To honour his wife, Mr Jones decided to build a Gothic castle in her memory. Not only did the gentleman pay for its construction; he project-managed it himself. If there had been a television series called *Grand Designs* in the eighteenth century William Jones and his castle would have made an interesting programme.

According to accounts kept by Jones, the notable architect John Nash was involved in the planning, but most of the design work was done by John Davenport, a Welsh garden designer who specialised in the Gothic style. Davenport also designed the grounds for Clytha Park. The site chosen for the castle was a hill visible from the Clytha House. Mr Jones wanted the monument to be a focal point of the estate. Work started on Clytha Castle, near Abergavenny (*Y Fenni*) in 1790 and the detailed records of the construction, written in Jones' own hand, still exist. Rendered local

Clytha Castle, a folly built by William Jones
in memory of his dead wife

rubble was used together with stone transported from Bath to finish the battlements, mullions and lintels. The L-shaped castle included towers and curious crenellated walls that sloped upwards to meet in the centre of the asymmetric façade. To improve the view of the castle, a ha-ha – a disguised wall to keep out animals – was dug at the front.

It took William Jones and his workmen two years to build Clytha Castle. When it was finished he ordered Gothic furniture from Mayhew and Ince, a fashionable London company. Purchases of expensive French china, silk and paintings were also recorded in his ledger. As well as serving as a monument, Clytha Castle would be a place to visit, take tea and enjoy. However, not wanting to forget his wife,

William Jones added a plaque to the front of the castle which reads:

This Building was erected in the year 1790 by
WILLIAM JONES of Clytha House Esq
Fourth Son of JOHN JONES
of Lanarth Court Monmouthshire Esq and
Husband of ELIZABETH the last surviving Child
of Sir WILLIAM MORGAN of Tredegar KB
and GrandDaughter of the most Noble WILLIAM
Second Duke of Devonshire
It was undertaken for the purpose of relieving a mind
sincerely afflicted by the loss of a most
excellent Wife whose Remains were deposited
in Lanarth Church Yard A.D: 1787
and to the Memory of whose virtues
this Tablet is dedicated.

In the nineteenth century Mr Jones' descendants added extra rooms and turned Clytha Castle into estate cottages, housing three tenant families. Some of the rooms were, however, retained for use by the Herbert family; the Jones family changed their name in 1862.

By 1948 the castle was empty and in 1950 Gwladys Herbert turned ownership of the castle over to the Welsh Office. They in turn passed it on the National Trust. Today, the castle is leased by The Landmark Trust, which specialises in saving distressed historic buildings. Since acquiring the castle in 1973, extensive repairs and renovations have returned the building to its former glory. Today, Clytha Castle is used for holiday rentals and can accommodate up to six people in mock-Gothic splendour, a fitting use for such an unusual building.

59

John Renie's Grave
Monmouth

On 8 October 2005 a tombstone in the churchyard at St Mary's Priory Church, Monmouth (*Trefynwy*), was listed as a Grade II structure, indicating that it is a building of special interest, warranting every effort to preserve it. The headstone, which stands close to the church, was carved to mark the graves of John Renie, his wife and two sons.

Renie was born in Monmouth and worked as a painter and decorator in the town until he died aged thirty-three, in 1832. According to some accounts, Renie, a noted eccentric, wanted to confound the devil so that, when he passed away, his journey to heaven would be straightforward. In order to do so Renie decided, rather oddly, to carve his own tombstone. What he created was an intricate 'acrostic puzzle' containing 285 letters arranged to read, 'Here lies John Renie.'

To understand the inscription, readers have to start from an 'H' in the centre of the puzzle and follow the letters in any direction. According to mathematicians who have studied the puzzle, there are 32,032 different ways to read 'Here lies John Renie' on the headstone. It must have been a laborious job carving such an intricate pattern. No records exist to say how many times Renie accidentally chipped off a letter and

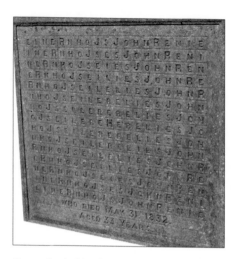

Starting from the 'H' in the centre, the tombstone contains more than 32,000 ways of reading 'Here lies John Renie'

had to start again with a new blank headstone.

Although the tombstone says 'Here lies John Renie', Renie and his family are actually buried elsewhere in the churchyard. In 1851, residents of nearby Whitecross Street began to die at an alarming rate and there were complaints of an unpleasant stench in the area. The stink was found to be coming from the churchyard where human remains had begun to emerge from the ground. Weathering and erosion, caused by the raised position of the graveyard, had worn away the topsoil exposing bodies of the deceased. The graveyard was closed to new burials and the remains reinterred. It was either then, or possibly later, that John Renie's headstone was moved to its current prominent position, next to the church, so that passing pedestrians might enjoy his puzzle.

We have no way of knowing where John Renie's soul ended up, but if honest work is truly rewarded in the afterlife, his labours carving a headstone to deceive the devil should have guaranteed St Peter would allow him through the pearly gates.

60

The Kymin
Monmouth

A painting of Philip Meakins Hardwick, in
Monmouthshire Museum, portrays him as a portly
gentleman who clearly enjoyed his food. During the
Georgian period, Hanoverian Royalty made over-
indulging fashionable. Having a large body was
considered stylish and an indication of one's wealth.
As a result of his gluttony and dissolute lifestyle, King
George IV was so obese that a crane, operated by
flunkeys, was installed in the royal bathroom at the
Brighton Royal Pavilion. Without it, the king was
unable to get into or out of the bath. A 1792 caricature
by James Gilray described George as 'A voluptuary
under the horrors of digestion'.

In keeping with the fashion, Mr Hardwick got
together with wealthy friends in 1794 and created the
Monmouth Picnic Club, sometimes also called the
Kymin Club. This exclusive club for gentlemen
included eight Members of Parliament. The Duke of
Beaufort, a prominent landowner, was also a leading
member.

Club members gathered weekly, 'for the purpose of
dining together and spending the day in a social and
friendly manner'. Instead of frequenting public dining
rooms or taverns, the members wanted a private
venue and started collecting money to build a

The Kymin, a gentlemens' luncheon club

*The Naval Temple,
restored in 2011, was
greatly admired
by Admiral Nelson*

banqueting hall suitable for such distinguished occasions. The location they chose was the summit of Kymin Hill, a mile east of Monmouth. Kymin had once been the site of a prehistoric hill fort and afforded the diners excellent long-distance views across nine counties.

The banqueting house, known as the Kymin, was a circular two-storey building with a kitchen on the ground floor and opulent dining room above. To take full advantage of the views, club members mounted a powerful telescope on the roof. Stables and a new road for the members' carriages were constructed to give better access. Later, a bowling green was laid out, together with a park so the gentlemen could enjoy the country air after their meals.

In 1800 the Kymin Club decided to build a temple to honour the Royal Navy and its glorious victories. Two years earlier the navy, commanded by Admiral Nelson, had annihilated a French fleet at the Battle of the Nile, forcing Napoleon Bonaparte to abandon his army in Egypt and return to France. It was a significant victory that removed a serious threat to British interests in the Middle East. The Battle of the Nile is regarded as one of the Royal Navy's most famous triumphs.

The temple is built in a classical style and commemorates sixteen famous British Admirals from the eighteenth century. Four plaques were hung on each of the four aspects of the temple giving details of the admirals and their battle honours. A bronze of Britannia depicted seated was mounted on the top of the structure. Traditionally, Britannia had been shown holding a spear but because the temple was recording naval battles the spear was replaced with a trident. The poem 'Rule Britannia' was turned into a popular song in 1740. When it was completed, the temple was dedicated by the Duchess of Beaufort, her father Admiral Boscowan being one of the naval officers celebrated on the monument.

In 1802, the hero of the time, Vice Admiral Horatio Nelson accompanied by his lover, Lady Hamilton, and her husband, Sir William Hamilton, visited Monmouth during a tour of south Wales. Their party arrived in the town by boat along the Wye, to the sound of celebratory cannon fire and rousing music from the town's brass band. They stayed in Monmouth and visited the Kymin, where they enjoyed a breakfast with club members. Visiting the Naval Temple, Nelson was reported to have been impressed and said, 'It was the only one of its kind erected to the Royal Navy in the Kingdom'. Three years later, in 1805, Nelson was killed at the Battle of Trafalgar, but another thirty-eight years passed before the famous column honouring him was erected in Trafalgar Square.

Following the demise of the Kymin Club, the Kymin passed into the ownership of Monmouthshire County Council who opened the park to the public. In 1902 the Kymin was given to the National Trust, who restored it to its former glory. In 2011, the trust announced an £85,000 restoration scheme would be undertaken to save the almost derelict temple. The restoration included replacing missing plaques, repairs to the roof, and commissioning a new statue of Britannia.

The temple was rededicated in August 2012. The ceremony was attended by Mrs Anna Tribe, the great-great-great-granddaughter of Admiral Nelson and Lady Hamilton. Mrs Tribe lives in Monmouthshire, is a recognised authority on her ancestor, and has presented lectures on Nelson at the National Maritime Museum in Greenwich. Most of Mrs Tribe's six children have been given the names Horatio or Horatia. Nelson and Lady Hamilton named their only child, a daughter, Horatia. Perhaps, because of interest by the gentlemen of Monmouth in naval achievements, the museum at Monmouth now contains one of the most important collections of Nelson memorabilia.

Today, the Kymin and the Naval Temple are fully restored and in the stewardship of the National Trust. The Kymin is available for private functions, including weddings, and both buildings are open to the public at certain times. Each year, runners participate in the 'Kymin Dash', a lung-bursting 7.5 mile race up the hill to the banqueting house and back to Monmouth School; something that Philip Meakins Hardwick would never have contemplated.

Heritage

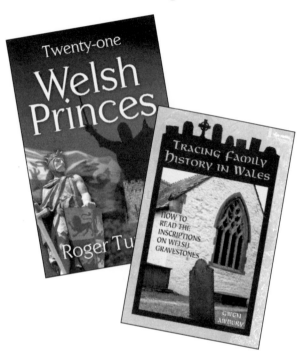

Visit our website for further information:
www.carreg-gwalch.com

Orders can be placed on our
On-line Shop